Tales from the Couch

WILLIAM MORROW

An Imprint of HarperCollins*Publishers*

TALES FROM THE COUCH

[Writers on Therapy]

EDITED BY JASON SHINDER

HarperCollins books may be purchased for educational, business, or
sales promotional use. For information please write: Special Markets
Department, HarperCollins Publishers Inc., 10 East 53rd Street,
New York, NY 10022.

FIRST EDITION

Designed by Kate Nichols

Printed on acid-free paper

Library of Congress Cataloging-in-Publication Data
Tales from the couch : writers on therapy / edited by Jason Shinder.
p. cm.
ISBN 0-380-97614-5
1. Psychoanalysis—Miscellanea.   2. Writers, American—
Psychological aspects.   I. Shinder, Jason, 1955–
RC506.T27   2000
616.89'17—dc21
00-041825

00 01 02 03 04 RRD 10 9 8 7 6 5 4 3 2 1

For Steven Bauer

and

for Dr. Jules Kerman

Psychotherapy was dubbed "the talking cure" almost at the moment of its inception by Anna O., its seminal patient. Freud's colleague, Josef Breuer, was treating Anna O. for a variety of symptoms that arose after her father's death. During the course of her therapy (in which Breuer used hypnosis to loosen her memory and her tongue), some of her symptoms were relieved when the memory was dislodged and expressed. As a result of studying Anna O. with Breuer, Freud observed (among a number of other key factors that would become elements of psychoanalysis) the importance of free association as a means of reaching the unconscious mind. It seems that Anna O. also recognized the importance of expressing her thoughts and referred to the treatment as "chimney sweeping."

—DR. ILANA RABINOWITZ,
Tales from a Traveling Couch

And the end of all our exploring
Will be to arrive where we started
And know the place for the first time.

— T. S. ELIOT,
Four Quartets

CONTENTS

CONTENTS

ACKNOWLEDGMENTS

This book would not have been possible without the assistance of Ruth Greenstein, Sharon Friedman, and Kelly Notaras. Chris Schelling and Katie Adams also played a critical role in seeing the book through to its final shape. Thanks also to Charlotte Abbott, Sophie Cabot Black, Lucie Brock Broido, Hamilton Cain, Tia Maggini, and Liz Rosenberg.

And thanks foremost to the contributors in this book, who accepted the challenge and opportunity to write about a very private and critical life experience.

INTRODUCTION

Can therapy change a person's life?

Many of the writers in this collection answer that question with a spirited and hard-fought-for *yes*. "Psychoanalysis has made me a finer writer, a fuller person," Ntozake Shange tells us. The "process . . . has allowed me to be so much more fully alive than I could have dreamed," Pam Houston declares. Even short-lived therapy (one or two sessions talking privately with a professional psychologist, counselor, or psychiatrist) can have a profound influence. "I realized I had come full circle," George Plimpton observes after brief therapeutic experiences more than fifty years apart.

The critical factor in almost all the effective therapy described in this book is the nature of the relationship between the writer and therapist. *It is the relationship that heals,* Carl Rogers declared, and almost every essay in this collection supports that axiom. Indeed, the nature and texture of the relationship between the writer/patient-talker and the therapist-listener becomes the driving force in the process of personal change. The therapy explored by the writers in this collection varies in form, perspective, ideology, technique (the more traditional Freudian approach as experienced by Adam Gopnik; the experimental

strategy of eye movement desensitization and reprocessing as undergone by Pam Houston), and content. Yet these differences surface as
secondary to the fundamental need for the writer/patient and therapist
to be bound together in some mutually valued, interesting, challenging, and gratifying dialogue—one that is supportive, honest, and
empathetic.

Of course, not everything about therapy works at first or at all.
E. Ethelbert Miller talks about the tendency to view therapists as
strangers without the understanding to offer much assistance. "How
could someone better guide me toward my own feelings than me?"
Other writers speak of the difficulties they had to overcome in order to
foster a successful therapeutic climate, especially that of finding and
building a trusting relationship with a therapist. "It took thirty years
of therapy with half a dozen psychiatrists," Susan Cheever writes,
before she could identify the characteristics of a successful patient-
therapist relationship. Diane Ackerman explores the circumstances
that often allow a sense of love and sexuality to flourish in a therapist's
office. "A friend asks what if she fell in love with her therapist." "You
would find yourself in a diabolically painful, unrequited relationship,"
Ackerman responds, "but you would also have the unique luxury of
being able to analyze your pain."

On one point, however, all of the anthologized writers agree: for
effective, genuine therapy to occur, one must risk the uncertainty, fear,
shame, and lack of control, real or imagined, that come with true and
ongoing self-revelation. This is especially important when encountering significant experiences—either painful *or* joyful—and it is not an
easy task. "Therapy teaches us how little of the world we control,"
David Mura writes. In many of the pieces, such self-revelation runs
along in a workaday fashion, featuring much pick-and-shovel fact-
finding and emotional exploration. Doug Bauer, Emily Fox Gordon,
Rebecca Walker, Susan Wood, Phillip Lopate, and Lucy Grealy,
among other writers in this collection, take us through this working
process in great detail. For other authors, such as Carole Maso, what
remains of this therapeutic process is highly charged threads of

encounters and dialogues that together seem to have a summary effect, condensing the experience to its basic elements of sense and memory.

No matter how talk therapy is recalled by these writers, however, each retelling eventually confirms a difficult and irreversible truth that the responsibility for one's life is, and always has been, in one's own hands. For all of the writers who experienced a significant benefit from therapy, it did not work unless they were working hard too; seeking out supportive friends; trading one therapist for another, more suitable one; accepting and forgiving imperfections in themselves and others (including the therapist); pursuing clarity again and again even when it is elusive and painful; bringing a persistent and rigorous desire for change to the therapeutic process.

In every essay the process of self-revelation and responsibility takes shape in two critical ways: the personal life of the writer and the private encounters between the writer and the therapist. In addition to sharing these intimate details, the writers here explore one other important factor: how psychotherapy has influenced their writing. Some express trepidation—will therapy strip away the secrets of the unconscious that fill their work with mystery and energy? The answer, for most, is a relieved no. Each of the writers eventually understands they can write through, and with, therapy, strengthening their levels of engagement with the issues of the self and the imagination. "The therapy session gives you an ideal area in which to attempt to say the most truth you can," Phillip Lopate writes. "It offers the personal essayist concrete practice for the achievement of candor." "Of the healing arts, therapy is surely the most literary, since it involves the telling and revision of a story," Mark Doty confirms.

And, as often in art, every story of truth-seeking talk therapy in this collection attempts to restore and strengthen passion and meaning to the concept of identity and love that each of us is destined and hoping for.

Tales from the Couch

ON THE SERENGETI

Rewriting a Life

Of the healing arts, therapy is surely the most literary, since it involves the telling and revision of a story. And of the literary arts, therapy's the oddest and most intimate, because the story is told for one listener only, and that listener becomes a collaborator in the shaping of the tale. No listener is ever asked to work harder, or to take more of the hand in the work of bringing order to the broken pieces of a narrative.

A tale is, after all, one of the things we are. Put it this way: we each operate out of an understanding of who we are and why we act as we do, an understanding based on an interpretation of the story of our lives—what we emphasize, what we suppress, how we "read" the tangled lines of motivation and desire that thread through a life. For most of us entering therapy, this personal narrative's in large part unexamined. The work of the therapist is to bring the story to the light, to help us examine how it has shaped us and how it might be retold.

Since our understandings are made of words, becoming self-aware means that we confront our own lives as a set of terms. I know what you're thinking: a writer *would* say that. But bear with me. I want to demonstrate something about the way the stories of our lives are first told to us, for us; to my mind, the work of therapy is a work of learning to wrest that act of narration into our own hands.

Writers understand this process intuitively, because it's familiar; we're used to confronting the puzzle of the story or poem that won't come right, wrestling it around, despairing, forgetting about it and then—that's it!—an understanding's reached, a new metaphor transforms the material, a new way of seeing makes it new. Perspective allows a different sort of freedom, which grants us new possibilities.

Revising a poem or story might take hours or days, weeks or even years, struggling and waiting for the insight that will lead to getting it right; the process brings an addictive mix of pleasure and frustration, challenge and resolution. This contained drama has the qualities of a serious game.

Revising your life is a whole other matter.

My first therapist was an unmitigated disaster. Call him Harry. He was a middle-aged guy with wiry white hair surrounding a shiny pink disk of a bald spot. He wore corduroy trousers held up by a belt with an elaborate buckle of hand-cast silver, convoluted and intricate tendrils of metal twirling together like the aftermath of some miniature automobile accident. He was fond of sporting a big medallion, too, a smaller cousin of the belt buckle, which hung from his neck on a leather cord and rested against his turtleneck sweater. (Need I mention this was 1976?)

Harry was a gestalt therapist, he said, and I didn't have the wit to inquire too deeply, scared to death as I was of the whole operation. He wrote poetry on the side. What I told him in my first session was that my marriage to Ruth presented problems for me because she was sometimes a difficult person, particularly when she drank. Which was true, but it was only a part of the truth. I felt nervous talking to him, as if I were representing myself to someone who was going to judge me, as if this were some perverse kind of job interview. Harry pulled a picture from a drawer in his desk, a drawing that could be seen either as two faces peering at one another or, if you did a little mental gymnastic and shifted your sense of figure and ground, a footed bowl full of fruit. "You see," he said, "there's another way to look at this."

Then he read me one of his poems—I'd told him that I made my living as a writer, teaching poetry workshops in public schools—and asked me my opinion of his writing. I should have known right then that I was in trouble.

But I didn't, because in fact I was entirely occupied with what I was saying to Harry, and what I *wasn't* saying to him, wasn't saying to myself; I was so busy damning myself I hadn't taken any time to evaluate *him* at all. I wasn't saying that Ruth's drinking was almost constant, and her behavior when she drank frightening and destructive; I wasn't saying that I felt trapped in a marriage I never should have gotten into in the first place; I wasn't saying that my desire lay in another direction entirely, toward other men. But I could barely say that to myself then, let alone say it to the obstreperously straight Harry, who wasn't really listening anyway.

But it isn't quite true that I couldn't say it to myself, since in fact my life had been wrapped around that particular piece of knowledge—like a young tree lashed to a stick which finally subsumes the brace into its own bark—since I was five years old and I went for a ride on the back of my sister's boyfriend's motorcycle. Jerry was all of eighteen, wavy-haired, shirtless, muscled, and when I sat behind him and put my arms around his bare stomach I understood something, even as my torso filled up with butterflies and my brain started to behave like one of those Fizzies they used to sell in the '50s. A Fizzie was a flavored disk you dropped into a glass of water; it would dissolve like a colorful version of an Alka-Seltzer, staining the liquid red or pink or turgid orange. Jerry made me feel dropped into a depth I couldn't fathom, and from then on, men's bodies would be for me a compelling source of mystery and power.

But it's dizzying, what we can know and not know, what we can see and yet hide from ourselves in the act of hiding from others. It's possible to live as if truth might be held at some remove from the stuff of daily life; truth was something seen, fleetingly, something always there, yet never allowed to breathe in the open. I held my real desires at such a distance that the result was to hollow out the life devoted to the denial and submersion of that truth. The central fact of feeling denied, no feeling seems quite real, and so I lived a broad, complete, false life. I had a kitchen full of elaborate implements, an upright piano painted white, which my wife used to play at our frequent parties; I had cats and a garden; I had a study high in the attic of our house where I'd go at night to write. Into the late hours the lamp up there would shine over the leaves of our big crabapple trees, bright on the ceiling of the sloping room under the eaves where I might be working on one of my veiled poems full of displaced feeling (now, I can see, all rage or thwarted longing). Or pulling out the *Playgirl* centerfold I'd hidden, my private little altarpiece of shame and desire. Or even, if I let myself, weeping.

Life in the closet is like the reflection on the surface of a plate glass window: it looks real, it has color, movement, but there's not an ounce of blood in it. Flesh is not flesh; the body doesn't seem real to itself.

And so I'd come to Harry in a kind of emotional paralysis. Something had to change, though in truth I could not imagine what or how. I was utterly stalled; I had the imaginative capacity to register the paucity of the state I'd come to, but not the imaginative capability to see what might lie ahead. I believed—I still believe—that the ability to imagine a change, another way to proceed, would have to begin with an understanding of the past.

But Harry wasn't interested in history. "We're only here today," he roared, "so let's talk about now!" If we were going to work on my relationship, he insisted, then Ruth would need to be there, too.

And Ruth agreed, a bit reluctantly, but I suppose she must have known how much had come between us, how we seemed to be making gestures toward one another across a widening distance, and how little genuine speech was making it across that gulf. It hadn't always been that way. We'd met when I was seventeen, and though twenty years lay between us, I neither knew that then nor felt a gap between us. She simply never told me how old she was, and when I asked she spun an elaborate tale about a drunken doctor who'd delivered her one stormy night in backcountry Louisiana, forgetting to make out a birth certificate, and a forgetful mother too unconcerned with worldly things to keep up with her daughter's age. Right. At seventeen, I found such fictions charming and magnetic. If her dissembling was a verbal version of Blanche DuBois covering her lamps with silk scarves to soften the light to something kinder, then I liked that all the more. I liked her poetry and her dreaminess, her exotic mix of bohemianism and Southern propriety. She'd been married previously, and driven her husband's TR4 right up the steps of the university library; she'd been arrested for wading in the college fountains late at night. She adored silver spoons, bone china, and the poetry of Sylvia Plath.

I hadn't exactly planned to marry her. But we'd begun an affair, my first, after we'd met at a poetry reading at the university. So far I'd only had sex with men, in the rest room in the Liberal Arts building, where I'd duck out of my boring art history lectures, far more compelled by the possibility of encountering a real Greek torso than looking at ancient ones. Although the quest for sex compelled me, the circumstances—the smell of the urinals and of chemical disinfectants, the ravenous appetites of the older men who knelt, mouth to the glory hole on the other side of the stall—filled me with shame and confusion. Was this what my life was going to be?

I told Ruth I was "bisexual," which was an accommodation I was attempting to make to my own sense of difference. It was 1971, after all, and there was a fashionable tolerance for notions of androgyny, though not for homosexuality. I had, in fact, never met a self-proclaimed gay person. I didn't have any sense that there was a life out there for me to join; I thought if I gave in to what I wanted, my future lay with the men I'd met hanging out in the stalls at Liberal Arts, and since I couldn't see them in any wider context, I imagined a future of lonely rooms, odors of dissatisfaction, disconnection, disinfectant. I didn't tell her about these guys, just about my desire, and she dismissed my claim, saying she didn't believe me, that I must be confused—I was, after all, sexually ardent with her—and we didn't speak about it again for nearly a decade.

And I did feel that I was in love with her, and her mysteries intrigued, and—oh! I could have sex with a woman; I could be someone at least in the *direction* of who I was supposed to be, and thus I didn't have to be so afraid of myself. So we began to live together, and then, to my parents' admixture of shock and relief (I was probably crazy but at least I wasn't queer), we married, because I was too passive to tell her I didn't want to. We had the ceremony in our apartment, with a Universalist minister who slipped the words "till death do us part" back into the ceremony, though I'd asked him to take them out. We filled the apartment with oleander flowers picked from the neighbors' gardens and stuffed in empty wine bottles; our friends sang and played the guitar; on the balcony we cut the cake I'd made myself, decorated with real flowers, and I spilled champagne all over my starched white Mexican wedding shirt.

Over the six years between the wedding party and our first visit to Harry's chocolate-brown office, with its big earth-colored prints decking the walls above stuffed vinyl chairs, our sense of making a life together had moved from something genuine to a kind of elaborate code of conventions. I knew everything Ruth wanted me to feel, understood who she wanted me to be, and felt determined to appear as such as much as I could. That's what I had agreed to by marrying her, wasn't it? But she wasn't happy, either; I could measure her misery by the volume of empty bottles on our back porch, because the state's new bottle-return law meant that every empty wine and whiskey and cognac bottle went back to the store, and one day, loading the clanking sacks into the car, I'd suddenly let myself see the absurd, horrifying number of them. And I'd seen her walking home from school hand in hand with one of her male students—another eighteen-year-old, another eager young poet!—raptly involved in an intimacy that must have provided some sense of connection I no longer could.

But who could get at any of this with Harry? I talked about Ruth. Ruth talked about me. She was far more poised than I was, since it was my anger, my fear that had brought us here; she presented herself as not needing or wanting anything to change, except that she wished I made more money in my freelance work, since she worried so much about money, being the one who made more of it in her job as a college teacher. And maybe it did anger her that she felt she was the responsible one, the breadwinner, since really she'd rather a man did that. I said she "got crazy" when she drank, not realizing that I'd chosen the one word that would drive Harry nuts. He wheeled around in his chair and snapped, "How dare you call her crazy! You don't even have a job!"

That was the end of whatever trust I'd extended to Harry; even I could see that therapy wasn't supposed to be like this. But it wasn't the end of the session. Harry considered our angers, suggested that we think about the relative proportions of our love for each other versus our troubles, and suggested we take the following actions: we were each to save our excrement, in a plastic bag, and when we had enough we were to get into the shower together, naked, and smear each other with our shit, so that we'd understand what we'd been doing to each other.

Harry sat back in his "pleather" chair, smiling, fingering his big medallion, happy that he'd shocked us, as though now we'd see.

And that was our last visit to Harry.

After that things sank back into what had become normal for us, our routine: I wrote and cooked and devoted myself to quitting smoking; Ruth read and played hymns on the piano and drank cognac. We stepped gingerly around the notion of therapy, as if it weren't for us, as if we had no choice but to fulfill the terms of the contract we'd entered into, which was bigger than both of us. "If you ever left me," she used to like to say, taking a drag on her long, brown More cigarette and turning her eyes somewhere toward heaven, "I'd kill myself."

And so the status quo was preserved, for a while, in part because living with Ruth increasingly became my job; as she drank more steadily, I found myself making sure her cigarettes were put out, her clothes taken to the cleaners, and those mornings when she couldn't teach I'd go and cover her classes myself—even noting, with an odd kind of pleasure I wouldn't let myself look at too closely—that her students seemed glad to see me. And the more I busied myself taking care of her, the less I had to attend to my own needs.

Though they rankled, and they roiled beneath the surface; desire too long denied sours, turns inward, spreading a sort of poison. I didn't know how truly out-of-plumb my life had become till I went to graduate school, to a low-residency writing program that only demanded I be away from home ten days each winter and summer. Ten days were enough to shake me to the core; suddenly I was spending all day, every day, with writers, people who talked about their lives, who examined their feelings and their motivations, and I understood with a shock bordering on panic that my inner life had become shrunken and withered. I'd been starving myself, because I'd been denying my desire. Isn't longing a sort of wellspring, a current that carries us forward into the adventure of our lives? Away from home, from my steadying job of faking it, taking care of a person both increasingly dependent and increasingly resentful, who was I? A person startlingly lacking in interior resources, in self-awareness. My peers were writing real poems, full of a struggle to understand, filled with engagement with experience, and I didn't have a clue where to begin. I felt like a small, scared thing, as if I'd stopped, at seventeen, when I took the wrong turn.

When I came home, after those first terrible ten days away, I said to Ruth, *If we're going to stay together we're going into therapy.* I offered no out. A friend whom I'd told about the Harry debacle recommended her therapist, who worked in an office with another woman. They saw couples together. We made an appointment.

In that first session with Diana and Bev my life began to change, though I couldn't see it then. The office was welcoming, with potted ficus and comfortable chairs and the ever-ready box of Kleenex, and though the therapists turned out to be two alert, bright-faced women in their early thirties, eager to find out who we were, I felt somehow submerged. I had the sensation that their sunny room was in fact filled with water, that it was hard for me to speak with so much liquid pressing against me, and that when my words came out they had that weird quavery sound your voice makes in your own ears when you try to talk at the bottom of a swimming pool. I might have been gesturing boldly, signaling from down in my depths that I wanted somebody please to hear me.

Every week we'd go to the office out in the suburbs on the edge of town, and every week Diana and Bev would work very hard. The method was this: Diana was basically "attached" to Ruth, Bev to me, so that each of us had a kind of ally. They would listen, try to restate what we'd said so we could each see if that was really what we meant, and then negotiate with the other parties, seeking response. There was something cumbersome about having a pair of mediators between us, but a kind of safety was granted, too. There were eight ears in that room, and didn't that mean that one's feelings were not only heard but mediated through an intervening buffer?

The only problem was that I began to feel safe, while Ruth did not. Our conversations very quickly arrived at the subject of alcohol, and Ruth steadfastly refused to acknowledge any problem. I was just paranoid, she asserted, because my mother had been alcoholic; I couldn't let her take a relaxing drink without thinking of addiction. We went round and round. Ruth's defenses were so bristling and numerous that even Diana didn't quite seem able to maintain her role as ally. Finally, we negotiated a deal: Ruth would restrict herself to "a glass or two" of wine a day, just while we worked on our problems. Even the stubbornly persistent Diana couldn't get her to narrow it to one.

But even after the hours we spent forging this agreement, Ruth couldn't do it. I don't think she tried—since it would have taken such a heroic act of will to resist that pull? Since getting sober would mean she'd have to look at us as we were?

We'd go to therapy and talk about other things, and then at some point Bev or Diana would say, "Let's check in on that agreement we made about alcohol." And Ruth would evade the question, or answer vaguely. The second or third time this happened, Diana insisted on an answer, a clear one, and finally Ruth said, "Yes, I have stuck to our agreement." Something sagged in me, though I couldn't have explained what it was. I said, "That's not true. How can you say you haven't been drinking?" Ruth stonewalled, not a crack in the armor, and that's where we left it. When I got home from work that evening, she was drunk in her favorite velvet chair. I walked past her, up to my study at the top of the house, and I lay down on a rag rug on the floor and started to weep. I found that I could not stop, that my grief felt bottomless, endless, and then my hands and then my arms went numb, dead. They frightened me; why did my body seem to be shutting down, refusing to move?

The next day I called Bev, and she asked to see me by myself. "It was probably a good thing," she said, "that your arms wouldn't move. Your body was protecting you; it wouldn't let you hurt Ruth or yourself." As we spoke, I understood that sagging feeling, that sense of collapse: I had been coming to the sessions in good faith, I'd been working at this with the belief that it might make things better. And I'd been working at it alone.

So Ruth began to see Diana by herself, and I to see Bev on my own. They suggested that at this point the issues were such that we'd be better off working independently. We could all come back together later. Ruth's response was mixed; what I saw as pointed honesty in Diana she viewed as confrontational. But she still seemed to want someone to talk to, someone who held out the unqualified attention and interest Diana offered.

I, on the other hand, felt I'd been given a gift so large I didn't quite know how to open it. Bev was an acutely good listener; there was a feeling intelligence to her responses that made me feel deeply seen—both supported and challenged to see more clearly myself. She knew exactly how to listen for the feeling inside any statement, and to mirror that feeling back to me. Then she could always take things a step further, which made me understand that therapy can't ever stop at just support, at "You sound very angry." The work must always go a step further, to point to another way of seeing, another possibility for understanding. What Harry was trying to do with that silly drawing of faces and fruit bowls, Bev did with the real stuff of experience. My feelings honored, validated, I was ready to hear what I otherwise couldn't have accepted, which was that there might be another understanding to replace the one that was ensuring my misery.

She was prepared to push just enough. One day, early on in our sessions, she asked, "What about your life now wouldn't you change?" I, who was used to having an answer for everything, suddenly had nothing to say. The silence widened. I began to understand how very much work I had to do, how wrong I'd allowed all my circumstances to become, how flimsy my defenses and denials really were. I shocked myself with my inability to answer.

Bev encouraged me to tell my life, and she collaborated actively in the process, mostly through questions that invited me to feel and think my way further into the story. Unlike Harry she was voraciously interested in the past, and together we spent hours talking through my history. It seems absurd now to think that I didn't know how to connect my childhood and my adult life—the connections seem so obvious! But nothing's obvious till you see it yourself, and the fact that a problem is right in front of your face does not necessarily make the answer any easier to find.

My life had never seemed coherent to me before; storytelling is an act of framing and forging connections. The fact that both "frame" and "forge" have connotations of falsehood is no accident, because stories are made; they are artifices that pluck shape out of the stream of things.

This is the version of the story Bev and I composed: My mother was a mercurial woman, a frustrated painter who turned to booze when I was a teenager and, unable to stop, drank till she destroyed herself. My father was a rather passive man who felt he had no power in relation to his wife's drinking; he tried merely to avoid conflict, smooth things over as much as possible. He bought the booze, listened to her harangues, slipped me twenty bucks, and told me to get lost for a few days whenever she went on the rampage. Whatever his needs and feelings were—and who could say, really, since he didn't show them?—they were put on hold while he wrestled with the huge monster of my mother's habit.

That, I'd been instructed, was what marriage was: a sort of symbiosis, an unsatisfying union that had to do with a perennial, doomed attempt to rescue. I'd been a good little boy: cautious, observant, responsible. I'd felt, as children do, that whatever my parents suffered must center around me. I couldn't rescue my mother, and so I'd gone out and married the first woman I could find who resembled her: creative, conflicted, soaked in gin.

Scary shades of Oedipus! Was that what I'd done, just fulfilled a classic pattern? Well, more than one pattern, depending on the lens through which we chose to look. Yes, I'd married my mother. But hadn't I also been doggedly loyal to my father, trying to behave just as he had, modeling myself upon his self-erasure?

And what was in that for me? Because the truth was that the "enabler," the "co-dependent," always got something out of the bargain. (I was learning the vocabulary of twelve-step programs, which seemed so fresh and startling then, before such terms seeped into the lexicon our society uses to describe itself. Even in 1981 we acknowledged this perspective as simply one more lens, and how could there be too many ways of seeing?)

I got to hide from my feelings, of course: from my shameful desires, from the core of difference my parents had long ago apprehended in me, even though I tried to straighten up. Hadn't I been ashamed of myself since I was five, hadn't I known I wasn't who they wanted me to be?

And that wasn't all. I'd found in Ruth a safe harbor, those years ago, at a time when I was anything but safe at home. I'd reached a point where I couldn't have remained in my parents' house, and where would I have gone, with no skills and no job history and hair down to my waist? On that level, my pact with Ruth was economic, a way of taking care of myself. I learned from her the ways of the world: how to buy a shirt that fit, where to put the salad fork, how to get a credit card. In another life I'd have probably hooked up with an older gay man, who'd have been my guide into adulthood, but since I had no male mentor to guide my education I'd found the next best thing, a self-made woman with the depths and complications of a Tennessee Williams character. How well I'd come to know Miss Alma, and Violet Venable, and Alexandra del Lago!

And Ruth had gotten something out of this, too, hadn't she? Or at least gotten herself *into* something, rushing into a wedding with a boy of seventeen—well, all of eighteen when we actually tied the knot.

Bev and I turned these things over week after week, and our incremental understandings struck me with the force of the revelation. I began to write about my family in a way I'd never been able to before; my new poems startled me with their directness and emotional availability. Bev asked to read them, and we talked about the images I'd chosen, and their implications, and the interpretations of memory the poems posited. This made me feel more seen, and I began to feel, without ever quite saying it to myself, that I'd never been known like this. No one had seen me this clearly, because I hadn't let them, and because no one else would look at me outside the filter of their own needs. I was not a player in Bev's drama; this was a deeply disinterested relationship and therefore capable of a kind of intimacy that was unlike anything I had known.

Which is to say, she made me feel real, I who'd been a closeted shadow.

Thus my marriage teetered to a close. I think now that day when my arms froze themselves was a sort of ending, but there were other scenes, too. Because Ruth had been teaching the elliptical novels of Alain Robbe-Grillet, her students threw a party where everyone came dressed as characters in *Last Year at Marienbad,* each told to arrive at a specific time, like "8:17." I wore a tux and carried a pearl-handled pistol; Ruth, a long dress and a purple feather boa. Outrageously drunk, she wound up making out on the couch with a student, while I nervously chatted and fingered my weapon. This was my marriage, all right: a costume party fraught with hostile gestures, an imaginary garden with real toads in it. That much was familiar; the startling part was that, after I steadied my hapless wife and got her home and up the stairs and into bed—still clutching those bedraggled violet feathers—I went back to the party alone and had a perfectly fine time. I hadn't known I could do that.

Then I went to Africa. The trip was a gift, a fluke. I escorted a pair of teenagers through Kenya, hired because their grandmother, who'd given the boys this plum of a birthday present, didn't feel she was up to bouncing around in jitneys. But I was raring to go, and for a month I filled my gaze with fabulously plumed birds, with the poignant nobility of elephants, the ominous and intricate leather of sunning crocodiles. I loved it. Early one morning, toward the end of the trip, I showed up at the door of the lodge where we were staying on the edge of the Serengeti to meet the open-roofed van that took groups of visitors out into the bush. The sun wasn't even up yet, but the good-natured driver with beautiful pendulous earlobes stretched from heavy jewelry (removed during the months he worked at the lodge) drove me out onto the plain anyway.

The sun came up scarlet and eager over a plain milling with so much hurry it seemed the teeming center of the pulse of things: here were racing antelopes, lumbering wildebeest, the fleet and disreputable hyenas, a quick-hooved juggernaut of zebras, spiraled and raucous crowds of birds. Everything kicking up dust, everything squawking or grunting or striking the earth, all in dynamic motion, layers upon layers of life in all directions, fired by the gorgeous possibility of the morning, animated and red and on the rise.

And I thought, You don't have to be this unhappy.

So that's where my marriage ended, really, on the Serengeti Plain. Of course, there was a great deal of painful arranging, of planning and weeping, of accusation and recrimination. The worst of it was that she felt so deeply betrayed, and I could not expect her to see that in fact I didn't want to leave her, though I also wanted to leave with all my heart. I loved her, but we'd reached a point where that fact had nothing to do with how we needed to live, with what needed to happen next. And oddly, when I told Ruth about my African dawn, it was plain that she appreciated the story, the potency of the image, even if she didn't like where it led; she, too, was a writer, and understood how our images sometimes know more than we do, how the beauty of a narrative has an authority of its own. Even if it's a story about ourselves, one in which we appear in an unhappy light.

It took me a while to feel any of that animal exhilaration I'd glimpsed back in Kenya, since first there was so much sadness to be acknowledged. I'd wanted to make Ruth happy, as no one could, just as I'd wanted to please my mother, as no one could. I believe we both began with good intentions, deluded as we were, and we hadn't meant to cause each other pain. I didn't want things to come to this passage, this sense of our mutual failure, our helplessness in the face of truth—and yet there was something bracing in it, too, something so plainly honest, when nothing between us had felt genuine for a long time. In that sense of the genuine lay a seed of friendship, some remnant of what had brought us together in the first place besides need and trouble.

Leaving, I began to understand the incredible narcissism of the enabler, the one who thinks he's necessary. She didn't kill herself without me, of course, though for months I cringed every time I heard a siren. She didn't fall apart any more than she had been falling apart with me; and in fact there were plenty of other people she could find to step into my shoes, since finding helpers was one of Ruth's primary ways of operating in the world. I wasn't irreplaceable! Maybe I hadn't even been important, finally. Our separation propelled her into further therapy, further change.

And, my energies withdrawn from her needs, I began to see that I no longer had that useful distraction. What did I want? How would I deal with this whole new messy life of my own choosing, and what if I screwed up, what if my new gay life was miserable? I'd be responsible for that myself, wouldn't I, and there wouldn't be a soul but me to blame. That is, I'd be an adult.

I don't believe we are ever truly independent beings who call all our own shots, write our own novels. It's more complicated than that; something more like taking the terms and phrases and characteristics written onto you and learning to use them, to shape them, to effect a collaboration between who you are and who you want to be. People aren't blank pages who get to rewrite themselves from scratch, and thank goodness for that. The things that scar and shape us are the things that make us beautiful, potentially, and certainly they are the things that make us ourselves. I learned irreplaceable things from my difficult parents; I learned irreplaceable things from Ruth. But the point of therapy is to learn not to be controlled by the forces that have shaped you, at least not entirely; understanding our histories allows us—slowly, with difficulty—to choose.

I haven't seen Bev for nearly twenty years, which saddens me, though I understand that we're not friends. Thinking of her now, I realize I hardly knew her at all, in the sense of knowing about her life, her interests and engagements. What I knew was our collaboration, her capacity to focus so generously and energetically on our work of understanding. Our last meeting was in fact not a session but lunch; we'd come to some point in our long conversation where we confronted, together, a mystery, trying to understand human resilience in the face of trouble, what it is that makes us sink to the bottom or rise up kicking and paddling to save ourselves. We'd sat in silence for a while, as if we were both looking into something unfathomable, something she didn't understand any better than I did. And that's when we became no longer "doctor and patient" but two people who'd taken their joint inquiry as far as they could. That's where therapy ends, isn't it, where stories do? Only so much of experience can be contained; the world's always larger than our understanding of it, and thus artist and client and therapist alike must arrive at a certain humble sense of limit. We tell what we can, we make our provisional understandings until it's time for the next revision. And I was completely broke anyway, with every penny going to my new apartment and my attempt to keep my old car alive. So we had a good-bye lunch, in which Bev told me she was moving to Texas, and I told her I was getting serious about heading for New York.

I'd like to see her now, to tell her that she has remained in many ways my truest literary collaborator. She nurtured my urge to do the difficult work of seeing into feeling; she helped me find the courage to look into experience and emotion I couldn't name and actually feel exhilarated by the work of trying to articulate what I saw. The work that has mattered most to me couldn't have happened without her, since she ushered me to the door of my real life, the life out of which poems arise: joy and grief, passion and delight felt through and through, all the way to the core. Which is only possible when we can live out our complicated, nearly untellable selves without the frozen frame of false definitions the closet provides, when we can freely have access to the facts of our own desires. That is what I glimpsed in Africa, I think, on the morning when the still-cool air filled with cries.

ADAM GOPNIK

MAN GOES TO SEE
A DOCTOR

Lately, a lot of people in New York—why, I'm not entirely sure—
have been sending me clippings about the decline and fall of psychoanalysis. Most of the reasons given for its disappearance make sense:
people are happier, busier; the work done by the anti-Freudian skeptics has finally taken hold of the popular imagination, so that people
have no time for analytic longueurs and no patience with its mystifica-
tions. Along with those decline-and-fall pieces, though, I've also been
sent—and in this case I don't entirely want to know why—a lot of
hair-raising pieces about mental illness and its new therapies: about
depressions, disasters, hidden urges suddenly (or brazenly) confessed
and how you can cure them all with medicine. Talking is out, taking
is in. When I go back to New York, some of my friends seem to be lay-
ered with drugs, from the top down, like a pousse-café: Rogaine on
top, then Prozac, then Xanax, then Viagra. . . . In this context, my
own experience in being doctored for mental illness seems paltry and
vaguely absurd, and yet, in its way, memorable.

I was on the receiving end of what must have been one of the last,
and easily one of the most unsuccessful, psychoanalyses that have ever
been attempted—one of the last times a German-born analyst, with a
direct laying on of hands from Freud, spent forty-five minutes twice a

week for six years discussing, in a small room on Park Avenue decorated with Motherwell posters, the problems of a "creative" New York
neurotic. It may therefore be worth recalling, if only in the way that it
would be interesting to hear the experiences of the last man mesmerized or the last man to be bled with leeches. Or the last man—and
there must have been such a man as the sixteenth century drew to a
close and the modern age began—to bring an alchemist a lump of lead
in the sincere belief that he would take it home as gold.

So it happened that on a night in October, 1990, I found myself sitting in a chair and looking at the couch in the office of one of the oldest, most patriarchal, most impressive-looking psychoanalysts in New
York. He had been recommended to me by another patient, a twenty-
year veteran of his couch. The choice now presents itself of whether to
introduce him by name or by pseudonym, a choice that is more one of
decorum than of legal necessity (he's dead). To introduce him by name
is, in a sense, to invade his privacy. On the other hand, not to introduce
him by name is to allow him to disappear into the braid of literature in
which he was caught—his patients liked to write about him, in masks,
theirs and his—and from which, at the end, he was struggling to break
free. He had, for instance, written a professional article about a well-
known patient, in which the (let's say) playwright who had inspired
the article was turned into a painter. He had then seen this article, and
the disputes it engendered, transformed into an episode in one of the
playwright's plays, with the playwright-painter now turned into a
novelist, and then the entire pas de deux had been turned by a colleague into a further psychoanalytic study of the exchange, with the
occupations altered yet again—the playwright-painter-novelist now
becoming a poet—so that four layers of disguise (five, as I write this)
gathered around one episode in his office. "Yes, but I received only one
check" was his bland response when I pointed this out to him.

His name, I'll say, was Max Grosskurth, and he had been practic-
ing psychoanalysis for almost fifty years. He was a German Jew of a
now vanishing type—not at all like the small, wisecracking, scared
Mitteleuropean Jews that I had grown up among. He was tall, com-

manding, humorless. He liked large, blooming shirts, dark suits, heavy handmade shoes, club ties. He had a limp, which, in the years when I knew him, became a two-legged stutter and then left him immobile, so that our last year of analysis took place in his apartment, around the corner from the office. His roster of patients was drawn almost exclusively from among what he liked to call creative people, chiefly writers and painters and composers, and he talked about them so freely that I sometimes half expected him to put up autographed glossies around the office, like the ones on the wall at the Stage Deli. ("Max—Thanks for the most terrific transference in Gotham! Lenny.") When we began, he was eighty, and I had crossed thirty.

I've read that you're not supposed to notice anything in the analyst's office, but that first evening I noticed it all. There was the couch, a nice Charles Eames job. On one wall there was a Motherwell print— a quick ink jet—and, opposite, a framed poster of one of the Masaccio frescoes in Santa Maria del Carmine in Florence. I was instantly impressed. The two images seemed to position him (and me) between Italian humanism, in its first, rocky, realistic form, at one end, and postwar New York humanism, in its jumpy, anxiety-purging form, at the other. On a bookshelf beside him were nothing but bound volumes of a psychoanalytic journal, rising to the ceiling. (He had edited that journal for a time. "Let me give you some counsel," he said to me much later. "Editing never means anything.")

He was lit by a single shaded bulb, just to his left, in that kind of standing brass lamp with a long arcing neck. This put his face in a vaguely sinister half light, but, with his strong accent and the sounds of traffic out on Park Avenue and a headlight occasionally sweeping across the room, the scene had a comforting European melancholia, as though directed by Pabst.

Why was I there? Nothing interesting: the usual mixture of hurt feelings, confusion, and incomprehension that comes to early-arriving writers when the thirties hit. John Updike once wrote that, though the newcomer imagines that literary New York will be like a choir of angels, in fact it is like the Raft of the Medusa—and he was wrong about this only in that the people on the Raft of the Medusa still have hope. In New York, the raft has been adrift now for years, centuries, and there's still no rescue boat in sight. The only thing left is to size up the others and wait for someone to become weak enough to eat.

I spilled out my troubles; told him of my sense of panic, anxiety, perhaps wept. He was silent for a minute—not a writer's minute, a real one, a long time.

"Franz Marc was a draftsman of remarkable power," he said at last, the first words of my analysis. His voice was deep and powerful, uncannily like Henry Kissinger's: not quacky, pleading Viennese but booming, arrogant German.

The remark about Franz Marc was not *quite* apropos of nothing— he knew me to be an art critic—but very near. (Franz Marc was the less famous founder of the German Expressionist movement called Der Blaue Reiter; Kandinsky was the other.) He must have caught the alarmed look in my eyes, for he added, more softly, "There are many worthwhile unexplored subjects in modern art." Then he sat up in his chair—swallowed hard and pulled himself up—and for a moment I had a sense of just how aged he was.

"You put me in mind," he said—and suddenly there was nothing the least old in the snap and expansive authority of his voice—"you put me in mind of Norman Mailer at a similar age." (This was a reach, or raw flattery; there is nothing about me that would put anyone in mind of Norman Mailer.) " 'Barbary Shore,' he thought, would be the end of him. What a terrible, terrible, terrible book it is. It was a great blow to his narcissism. I recall clearly attending dinner parties in this period with my wife, an extremely witty woman, where everyone was mocking poor Norman. My wife, an extremely witty woman . . ." He looked at me as though, despite the repetition, I had denied it; I tried to look immensely amused, as though reports of Mrs. Grosskurth's wit had reached me in my crib. "Even my wife engaged in this banter. In the midst of it, however, I held my peace." He rustled in his chair, and now I saw why he had sat up: he suddenly became a stiff, living pillar, his hands held before him, palms up—a man holding his peace in the middle of banter flying around the dinner table. A rock of imperturbable serenity! He cautiously settled back in his chair. "Now, of course, Norman has shown great resourcefulness and is receiving extremely large advances for his genre studies of various American criminals."

From the six years of my analysis, or therapy, or whatever the hell it was, there are words that are as permanently etched in my brain as the words "E pluribus unum" are on the nickel. "Banter" and "genre studies" were the first two. I have never been so grateful for a *mot juste* as I was for the news that Mrs. Grosskurth had engaged in banter, and that Norman Mailer had made a resourceful turn toward genre studies. Banter, that was all it was: criticism, the essential competitive relations of writers in New York—all of it was *banter,* engaged in by extremely witty wives of analysts at dinner parties. And all you had to do was . . . refuse to engage in it! Hold your peace. Take no part! Like him—sit there like a rock and let it wash over you.

And then there was the wacky perfection of his description of the later Mailer, with its implications of knowing (not firsthand certainly; Mailer, as far as I know, had never been his patient) the inside story: he had, under stress, found appropriate genre subjects. American criminals. The whole speech, I thought, was so profound that it could be parsed and highlighted like one of those dog-eared assigned texts you find on the reserve shelf in undergraduate libraries: Artists suffered from *narcissism,* which made them susceptible to *banter,* which they could overcome by *resourcefulness,* which might lead them to—well, to take up *genre studies.* ("Genre studies," I was to discover, was Grosskurthese for "journalism." He often indulged in strangely Johnsonian periphrases: once, talking about Woody Allen, he remarked, "My wife, who was an extremely witty woman, was naturally curious to see such a celebrated wit. We saw him in a cabaret setting. I recall that he was reciting samples of his writings in a state of high anxiety." It took me days of figuring—what kind of reading had it been? a kind of Weimar tribute evening?—to realize that Dr. and Mrs. Grosskurth had gone to a nightclub and heard the comedian's monologue.)

I came away from that first session in a state of blissful suspended confusion. Surely this wasn't the way psychoanalysis was supposed to proceed. On the other hand, it was much more useful—and interesting, too—to hear that Norman Mailer had rebounded by writing genre studies than it was to hear that my family was weird, for that I knew already. I felt a giddy sense of relief, especially when he added, sardonically, "Your problems remind me of"—and here he named one of the heroes of the New York School. "Fortunately, you suffer neither from impotence nor alcoholism. That is in your favor." And that set the pattern of our twice- and sometimes thrice-weekly encounters for the next five years. He was touchy, prejudiced, opinionated, impatient, often bored, usually highhanded, brutally bigoted. I could never decide whether to sue for malpractice or fall to my knees in gratitude for such an original healer.

Our exchanges hardened into a routine. I would take the subway uptown at six-thirty; I would get out at Seventy-seventh Street, walk a couple of blocks uptown, and enter his little office, at the corner of Park Avenue, where I would join three or four people sitting on a bench. Then the door opened, another neurotic—sometimes a well-known neurotic, who looked as though he wanted to hide his face with his coat, like an indicted stockbroker—came out, and I went in. There was the smell of the air conditioner.

"So," he would say. "How are you?"

"Terrible," I would say, sometimes sincerely, sometimes to play along.

"I expected no less," he would say, and then I would begin to stumble out the previous three or four days' problems, worries, gossip. He would clear his throat and begin a monologue, a kind of roundabout discussion of major twentieth-century figures (Freud, Einstein, and, above all, Thomas Mann were his touchstones), broken confidences of the confessional, episodes from his own life, finally snaking around to an abrupt "So you see . . ." and some thunderously obvious maxim, which he would apply to my problems—or rather, to the nonexistence of my problems, compared with real problems, of which he'd heard a few, you should have been here then.

For instance: I raised, as a problem, my difficulty in finishing my book, in writing without a deadline. I raised it at length, circuitously, with emotion. He cleared his throat. "It is commonplace among writers to need extreme arousal. For instance, Martin Buber." I riffled through my card catalog: wasn't he the theologian? "He kept pornography on the lecture stand with him, in order to excite him to a greater performance as a lecturer. He would be talking about 'I and thou,' and there he would be shuffling through his papers, looking at explicit photographs of naked women." He shook his head. "This was really going very far. And yet Buber was a very great scholar. It was appropriate for his approach. It would not be appropriate for you, for it would increase your extreme overestimation of your own role."

Mostly, he talked about what he thought it took to survive in the warfare of New York. He talked about the major figures of New York literary life—not necessarily his own patients but writers and artists whose careers he followed admiringly—as though they were that chain of forts upstate, around Lake George, left over from the French and Indian War: the ones you visited as a kid, where they gave you bumper stickers. There was Fort Sontag, Fort Frankenthaler, Fort Mailer. "She is very well defended." "Yes, I admire her defenses." "Admirably well defended." Once, he mentioned a famous woman intellectual who had recently got into legal trouble: hadn't she been well defended? "Yes, but the trouble is that the guns were pointing the wrong way, like the British at Singapore." You were wrung out with gratitude for a remark like that. I was, anyway.

It was his theory, in essence, that "creative" people were inherently in a rage, and that this rage came from their disappointed narcissism. The narcissism could take a negative, paranoid form or a positive, defiant, arrogant form. His job was not to cure the narcissism (which was inseparable from the creativity) but, instead, to fortify it—to get the drawbridge up and the gate down and leave the Indians circling outside, with nothing to do but shoot flaming arrows harmlessly over the stockade.

He had come of age as a professional in the forties and fifties, treating the great battles of the golden age of New York intellectuals, an age that, seen on the couch—a seething mass of resentments, jealousies, and needs—appeared somewhat less golden than it did otherwise. "How well I recall," he would begin, "when I was treating"— and here he named two famous art critics of the period. "They went to war with each other. One came in at ten o'clock. 'I must reply,' he said. Then at four-thirty the other one would come in. 'I must reply,' he would say. 'No,' I told them both. 'Wait six months and see if anyone recalls the source of this argument.' They agreed to wait. Six months later, my wife, that witty, witty woman, held a dinner party and offered some pleasantry about their quarrel. No one understood; no one even remembered it. And this was in the days when *ARTnews* was something. I recall what Thomas Mann said. . . ." Eventually, abruptly, as the clock on the wall turned toward seven-thirty, he would say, "So you see . . . this demonstrates again what I always try to tell you about debates among intellectuals."

I leaned forward, really wanting to know. "What is that, Doctor?" I said.

"*No one cares*. People have troubles of their own. We have to stop now." And that would be it.

I would leave the room in a state of vague, disconcerted disappointment. *No one cares?* No one cares about the hard-fought and brutally damaging fight for the right sentence, the irrefutable argument? And: *People have troubles of their own?* My great-aunt Hannah could have told me that. *That* was the result of half a century of presiding over the psyches of a major moment in cultural history? And then, fifteen minutes later, as I rode in a cab downtown my heart would lift—would fly. That's right: *No one cares! People have troubles of their own!* It's O.K. That doesn't mean you shouldn't do it; it means you should do it, somehow, for its own sake, without illusions. Just write, just live, and don't care too much yourself. No one cares. It's just *banter*.

Sometimes his method of bringing me to awareness—if that was what he was doing—could be oblique, not to say bizarre. There was, for instance, the Volestein Digression. This involved a writer whose name was, shall we say, Moses Volestein. Dr. G. had once read something by him and been fascinated by his name. "What a terrible name," he said. "*Vole.* Why would a man keep such a terrible name?" His name didn't strike me as a burden, and I said so.

"You are underestimating the damage that this man's name does to his psychic welfare," he replied gravely. "It is intolerable."

"I don't think he finds it intolerable."

"You are wrong."

Then, at our next meeting: "Your resistance to my discussion of Volestein's name at our last session is typical of your extreme narcissistic overestimation. You continue to underestimate the damage a name like that does to the human psyche."

"Doctor, surely you overestimate the damage such a name does to the human psyche."

"You are wrong. His family's failure to change this name suggests a deep denial of reality." He pursued Volestein's name through that session and into the next, and finally I exploded.

"I can't believe we're spending another hour discussing Moses Volestein's funny name!" I said. "I mean, for that matter, some people might think my own name is funny."

He considered. "Yes. But your name is merely very ugly and unusual. It does not include a word meaning a shrewlike animal with unpleasant associations for so many people. It is merely very ugly."

And then I wondered. My name—as natural to me as the sound of my own breathing? I had volunteered that it might be peculiar, out of some mixture of gallantry and point-scoring. But my hurt was enormous. My wife, who had kept her own name when we married—out of feminist principle, I had thought—said, "Yes, when we met I couldn't believe it. I wouldn't go out with you for a week because of it." It was a shock as great as any I had received, and as salutary. Had he obsessed on Volestein with the intention of making me face Gopnik, in all its oddity, and then, having faced it, grasp some ironic wisdom? *I had a funny name*. And then the corollary: people could have funny names and go right on working. They might never even notice it. Years later, on-line, I found myself on a list of writers with extremely funny names—I suppose this is what people do with their time now that they are no longer in psychoanalysis—and I was, amazingly, happy to be there. So that was one score. Even your name could be absurd and you wouldn't know it. And the crucial addition: it didn't matter. Indifference and armor could get you through anything.

Sometimes Dr. Grosskurth would talk about his own history. He was born in Berlin before the First World War, at a time when German Jews were German above all. His mother had hoped that he would become a diplomat. But he had decided to study medicine instead, and particularly psychiatry; he was of that generation of German Jews who found in Freud's doctrines what their physicist contemporaries found in Einstein's. He had spoken out against the Nazis in 1933 and had been forced to flee the country at a moment's notice. One of his professors had helped him get out. (He was notably unheroic in his description of this episode. "It was a lesson to me to keep my big mouth shut" was the way he put it.) He fled to Italy, where he completed medical school at the University of Padua.

He still loved Italy: he ate almost every night at Parma, a restaurant nearby, on Third Avenue, and spent every August in Venice, at the Cipriani. One spring, I recall, I announced that my wife and I had decided to go to Venice.

He looked at me tetchily. "And where will you stay?" he asked.

"At this *pensione,* the Accademia," I said.

"No," he said. "You wish to stay at the Monaco, it is a very pleasant hotel, and you will have breakfast on the terrace. That is the correct hostel for you."

I reached into my pockets, where I usually had a stubby pencil, and searched them for a stray bit of paper—an American Express receipt, the back of a bit of manuscript paper—to write on.

"No, no!" he said, with disgust. My disorderliness was anathema to his Teutonic soul. "Here, I will write it down. Oh, you are so chaotic. Hand me the telephone." I offered him the phone, which was on a small table near his chair, and he consulted a little black book that he took from his inside right jacket pocket. He dialed some long number. Then, in a voice even deeper and more booming than usual—he was raised in a time when long-distance meant long-distance—he began to speak in Italian.

"Sì, sono Dottore Grosskurth." He waited for a moment—genuinely apprehensive, I thought, for the first time in my acquaintance with him—and then a huge smile, almost a big-lug smile, broke across his face. They knew him.

"Sì, sì," he said, and then, his voice lowering, said, "No," and something I didn't understand; obviously, he was explaining that Mrs. Grosskurth had died. *"Pronto!"* he began, and then came a long sentence beginning with my name and various dates in *giugno. "Sì, sì."* He put his hand over the receiver. "You wish for a bath or a shower?" he demanded.

"Bath," I said.

"Good choice," he said. It was the nearest thing to praise he had ever given me. Finally, he hung up the phone. He looked at the paper in his hand and gave it to me.

"There," he said. "You are reserved for five nights, the room has no view of the canal, but, actually, this is better, since the gondola station can be extremely disturbing. You will eat breakfast on the terrace, and there you will enjoy the view of the Salute. Do not eat dinner there, however. I will give you a list of places." And, on an "Ask Your Doctor About Prozac" pad, he wrote out a list of restaurants in Venice for me. (They were mostly, I realized later, after I got to know Venice a bit, the big old, fifties-ish places that a New York analyst would love: Harry's Bar, Da Fiore, the Madonna.)

"You will go to these places, order the spaghetti *vongole,* and then . . ."

"And then?"

"And then at last you will be happy," he said flatly.

He was so far from being an orthodox Freudian, or an orthodox anything, that I was startled when I discovered how deep and passionate
his attachment to psychoanalytic dogma was. One day, about three
years in, I came into his office and saw that he had a copy of *The New
York Review of Books* open. "It is very sad," he began. "It is very sad
indeed, to see a journal which was once respected by many people
descend into a condition where it has lost the good opinion of all rea-
sonable people." After a few moments, I figured out that he was referring to one of several much discussed pieces that the literary critic
Frederick Crews had written attacking Freud and Freudianism.

I read the pieces later myself and thought them incontrovertible.
Then I sat down to read Freud, for the first time—"Civilization and Its
Discontents," "Totem and Taboo," "The Interpretation of Dreams"—
and was struck at once by the absurdity of the arguments as arguments
and the impressive weight of humane culture marshaled in their support. One sensed that one was in the presence of a kind of showman, a
brilliant essayist, leaping from fragmentary evidence to unsupported
conclusion, and summoning up a whole body of psychological myth—
the Id, the Libido, the Ego—with the confidence of a Disney cartoonist drawing bunnies and squirrels. I found myself, therefore, in the
unusual position of being increasingly skeptical of the therapeutic
approach to which I fled twice a week for comfort. I finally got up the
courage to tell Grosskurth this.

"You therefore find a conflict between your strongest intellectual
convictions and your deepest emotional gratification needs?" he asked.

"Yes."

He shrugged. "Apparently you are a Freudian."

This seemed to me a first-rate exchange, honors to him, but I
couldn't let it go. My older sister, a professor of psychology at Berkeley, regarded Freud as a comic relic (I had told her about my adven-

tures in psychoanalysis), and in the midst of the *New York Review* debate she wrote one of the most devastating of the anti-Freud letters to the editor. She even made a passing, dismissive reference to the appeal of "figures of great personal charisma"—knew what *that* was about—and then stated, conclusively, that there was nothing to be said in defense of psychoanalysis that couldn't also be said in defense of magic or astrology. ("She is very well defended, your sister," Grosskurth said.)

On behalf of his belief, Grosskurth would have said—did say, though over time, if not in these precise words—that while Freud may have been wrong in all the details, his central insight was right. His insight was that human life is shaped by a series of selfish, ineradicable urges, particularly sexual ones, and that all the other things that happen in life are ways of toning down these urges and giving them an "acceptable" outlook. An actual, undramatic but perilous world of real things existed, whose essential character was its indifference to human feelings: this world of real things included pain, death, and disease, but also many things unthreatening to our welfare. His project—the Freudian project, properly understood—was not to tell the story of our psyche, the curious drawing-room comedy of Id and Ego and Libido, but just the opposite: to drain the drama from all our stories. He believed that the only thing to do with the knowledge of the murderous rage within your breast was not to mythologize it but to put a necktie on it and heavy shoes and a dark-blue woolen suit. Only a man who knew that, given the choice, he would rape his mother and kill his father could order his spaghetti *vongole* in anything like peace.

There was, however, a catch in this argument, or so I insisted in the third year of my analysis, over several sessions and at great length. Weren't the well-defended people he admired really the ones at the furthest imaginable remove from the real things, the reality, whose worth he praised so highly? Did Susan Sontag actually have a better grasp of things-as-they-are than anyone else? Would anybody point to Harold Brodkey as a model of calm appraisal of the scale of the world and the appropriate place of his ego in it? Wasn't the "enormous narcissistic overestimation" of which he accused me inseparable from the "well-defended, internalized self-esteem" he wanted me to cultivate? The people who seemed best defended—well, the single most striking thing about them was how breathtakingly out of touch they were with the world, with other people's feelings, with the general opinion of their work. You didn't just have to be armored by your narcissism; you could be practically entombed in it, so that people came knocking, like Carter at King Tut's tomb, and you'd still get by. Wasn't that a problem for his system, or, anyway, for his therapy?

"Yes," he said coldly.

"Oh," I said, and we changed the subject.

My friends were all in therapy, too, of course—this was New York—and late at night, over a bottle of red wine, they would offer one "insight" or another that struck me as revelatory: "My analyst helped me face the recurring pattern in my life of an overprotectiveness that derives from my mother's hidden alcoholism," or "Mine helped me see more clearly how early my father's depression shaped my fears," or "Mine helped me see that my reluctance to publish my personal work is part of my reluctance to have a child." What could I say? "Mine keeps falling asleep, except when we discuss Hannah Arendt's sex life, about which he knows quite a lot."

His falling asleep was a problem. The first few years I saw him, he still had a reasonably full schedule and our sessions were usually late in the day; the strain told on him. As I settled insistently (I had decided that if I was going to be analyzed I was going to be analyzed) into yet one more tiresome recital of grievances, injustices, anxieties, childhood memories, I could see his long, big, partly bald head nodding down toward the knot of his tie. His eyes would flutter shut, and he would begin to breathe deeply. I would drone on—"And so I think that it was my mother, really, who first gave me a sense of the grandiose. There was this birthday, I think my sixth, when I first sensed . . ."—and his chin would nestle closer and closer to his chest, his head would drop farther, so that I was looking right at his bald spot. There was only one way, I learned, after a couple of disconcerting weeks of telling my troubles to a sleeping therapist, to revive him, and that was to gossip. "And so my mother's relationship with my father reminds me—well, in certain ways it reminds me of what people have been saying about Philip Roth's divorce from Claire Bloom," I would say abruptly, raising my volume on the non sequitur.

Instantly, his head would jerk straight up, his eyes open, and he would shake himself all over like a Lab coming out of the water. "Yes, what are they saying about this divorce?" he would demand.

"Oh, nothing, really," I would say, and then I would wing it for a minute, glad to have caught his attention.

Unfortunately, my supply of hot literary gossip was very small. So there were times (and I hope that this is the worst confession I will ever have to make) when I would invent literary gossip on the way uptown, just to have something in reserve if he fell asleep, like a Victorian doctor going off to a picnic with a bottle of smelling salts, just in case. ("Let's see: what if I said that Kathy Acker had begun an affair with, oh, V. S. Pritchett—that would hold *anybody's* interest.") I felt at once upset and protective about his sleeping. Upset because it was, after all, my nickel, and protective because I did think that he was a great man, in his way, and I hated to see him dwindling: I wondered how long he would go on if he sensed that he was dwindling.

Not long ago, I read, in a book about therapy, a reference to a distinguished older analyst who made a point of going to sleep in front of his patients. Apparently, Grosskurth—for who else could it have been?—was famous for his therapeutic skill in falling asleep as you talked. It was tactical, even strategic.

Or was he just an old man trying to keep a practice going for lack of anything better to do, and doing anything—sleeping, booking hotel rooms, gossiping, as old men do—so that he would not have to be alone? Either limitlessly shrewd or deeply pathetic: which was it? Trying to answer that question was one of the things that kept me going uptown.

As we went on into our fourth and fifth years, all the other problems that I had brought to him became one problem, *the* New York problem. Should my wife—should we—have a baby? We agonized over it, in the modern manner. Grosskurth listened, silently, for months, and finally pronounced.

"Yes, you must go ahead and have a child. You will enjoy it. The child will try your patience repeatedly, yet you will find that there are many pleasures in child-rearing." He cleared his throat. "You will find, for instance, that the child will make many amusing mistakes in language."

I looked at him, a little dumbfounded—that was the best of it?

"You see," he went on, "at about the age of three, children begin to talk, and naturally their inexperience leads them to use language in surprising ways. These mistakes can really be *extremely* amusing. The child's errors in language also provide the kinds of anecdotes that can be of value to the parents in a social setting." It seemed an odd confidence on which to build a family—that the child would be your own, live-in Gracie Allen, and you could dine out on his errors—but I thought that perhaps he was only defining, so to speak, the minimal case.

So we did have the child. Overwhelmed with excitement, I brought him pictures of the baby at a week old. ("Yes," he said dryly, peering at my Polaroids, "this strongly resembles a child.") And, as my life was changing, I began to think that it was time to end, or anyway wind down, our relationship. It had been six years, and, for all that I had gained—and I thought that I had gained a lot: if not a cure, then at least enough material to go into business as a blackmailer—I knew that if I was to be "fully adult" I should break my dependence. And he was growing old. Already aged when we began, he was now, at eighty-five or -six, becoming frail. Old age seems to be a series of lurches, rather than a gradual decline. One week he was his usual booming self, the next week there was a slow deliberateness in his gait as he came to the office door. Six months later, he could no longer get up reliably from his chair, and once fell down outside the office in my presence. His face, as I helped him up, was neither angry nor amused, just doughy and preoccupied, the face of a man getting ready for something. That was when we switched our sessions to his apartment, around the corner, on Seventy-ninth Street, where I would ring the bell and wait for him to call me in—he left the door open, or had it left open by his nurse, whom I never saw. Then I would go inside and find him—having been helped into a gray suit, blue shirt, dark tie— on his own sofa, surrounded by Hofmann and Miró engravings and two or three precious Kandinsky prints.

About a month into the new arrangement, I decided to move to Europe to write, and I told him this, in high spirits and with an almost breathless sense of advancement: I was going away, breaking free of New York, starting over. I thought he would be pleased.

To my shock, he was furious—his old self and then some. "Who would have thought of this idea? What a self-destructive regression." Then I realized why he was so angry: despite all his efforts at fortification, I had decided to run away. Fort Gopnik was dropping its flag, dispersing its troops, surrendering its territory—all his work for nothing. Like General Gordon come to reinforce Khartoum, he had arrived too late, and failed through the unforgivable, disorganized passivity of the natives.

In our final sessions, we settled into a nonaggression pact. ("Have we stopped too soon, Doctor?" I asked. "Yes," he said dully.) We talked neutrally, about art and family. Then, the day before I was to leave, I went uptown for our last session.

It was a five-thirty appointment, in the second week of October. We began to talk, amiably, like old friends, about the bits and pieces of going abroad, visas and vaccinations. Then, abruptly, he began to tell a long, meandering story about his wife's illness and death, which we had never talked about before. He kept returning to a memory he had of her swimming back and forth in the hotel pool in Venice the last summer before her death.

"She had been ill, and the Cipriani, as you are not aware, has an excellent pool. She swam back and forth in this pool, back and forth, for hours. I was well aware that her illness was very likely to be terminal." He shook his head, held his hands out, dealing with reality. "As soon as she had episodes of dizziness and poor balance, I made a very quick diagnosis. Still, back and forth she swam."

He stopped; the room by now had become dark. The traffic on Seventy-ninth Street had thickened into a querulous, honking rush-hour crowd. He was, I knew, too shaky on his feet to get up and turn on the lights, and I thought that it would be indelicate for me to do it—they were his lights. So we sat there in the dark.

"Naturally, this was to be the last summer that we spent in Venice. However, she had insisted that we make this trip. And she continued to swim." He looked around the room, in the dark—the pictures, the drawings, the bound volumes, all that was left of two lives joined together, one closed, the other closing.

"She continued to swim. She had been an exceptional athlete, in addition to being, as you know, an extremely witty woman." He seemed lost in memory for a moment, but then, regaining himself, he cleared his throat in the dark, professionally, as he had done so many times before.

"So you see," he said, again trying to make the familiar turn toward home. And then he did something that I don't think he had ever done before: he called me by my name. "So you see, Adam, in life, in life . . ." And I rose, thinking, Here at our final session—no hope of ever returning, my bag packed and my ticket bought to another country, far away—at last, the truth, the point, the thing to take away that we have been building toward all these years.

"So you see, Adam, in retrospect . . ." he went on, and stirred, rose, on the sofa, trying to force his full authority on his disobedient frame. "In retrospect, life has many worthwhile aspects," he concluded quietly, and then we had to stop. He sat looking ahead, and a few minutes later, with a good-bye and a handshake, I left.

Now I was furious. I was trying to be moved, but I would have liked to be moved by something easier to be moved by. That was all he had to say to me, *Life has many worthwhile aspects?* For once, that first reaction of disappointment stuck with me for a long time, on the plane all the way to Paris. All these evenings, all that investment, all that humanism, all those Motherwell prints—yes, all that money, my money—for that? *Life has many worthwhile aspects?* Could there have been a more fatuous and arrhythmic and unmemorable conclusion to what had been, after all, *my* analysis, my only analysis?

Now, of course, it is more deeply engraved than any other of his words. In retrospect, life has many worthwhile aspects. Not all or even most aspects. And not beautiful or meaningful or even tolerable. Just *worthwhile,* with its double burden of labor and reward. Life has *worth*—value, importance—and it takes a while to get there.

I came back to New York about a year later and went to see him. A woman with a West Indian accent had answered when I called his number. I knew that I would find him declining, but still, I thought, I would find him himself. We expect our fathers to take as long a time dying as we take growing up. But he was falling away. He was lying on a hospital bed, propped up, his skin as gray as pavement, his body as thin and wasted as a tree on a New York street in winter. The television was on, low, tuned to a game show. He struggled for breath as he spoke.

He told me, very precisely, about the disease that he had. "The prognosis is most uncertain," he said. "I could linger indefinitely." He mentioned something controversial that I had written. "You showed independence of mind." He turned away, in pain. "And, as always, very poor judgment."

In New York again, five months later, I thought, I'll just surprise him, squeeze his hand. I walked by his building, and asked the doorman if Dr. Grosskurth was in. He said that Dr. Grosskurth had died three months before. For a moment I thought, Someone should have called me, one of his children. Yet they could hardly have called all his patients. ("But I was special!" the child screams.) Then I stumbled over to Third Avenue and almost automatically into Parma, the restaurant that he had loved. I asked the owner if he knew that Dr. Grosskurth had died, and he said yes, of course: they had had a dinner, with his family and some of his friends, to remember him, and he invited me to have dinner, too, and drink to his memory.

I sat down and began an excellent, solitary dinner in honor of my dead psychoanalyst—seafood pasta, a Venetian dish, naturally—and, in his memory, chewed at the squid. (He liked squid.) The waiter brought me my bill, and I paid it. I still think that the owner should at least have bought the wine. Which shows, I suppose, that the treatment was incomplete. ("They should have paid for your wine?" "It would have been a nice gesture, yes. It would have happened in Paris." "You are hopeless. I died too soon, and you left too early. The analysis was left unfinished.")

The transference wasn't completed, I suppose, but something—a sort of implantation—did take place. He is inside me. In moments of crisis or panic, I sometimes think that I have his woolen suit draped around my shoulders, even in August. Sometimes in ordinary moments I almost think that I have become him. Though my patience is repeatedly tried by my child, I laugh at his many amusing mistakes in language—I have even been known to repeat these mistakes in social settings. I refer often to the sayings of my wife, that witty, witty woman. On the whole, I would say that my years in analysis had many worthwhile aspects.

REBECCA WALKER

WRITING WITHOUT BENITO

After almost ten years of therapy, six months ago I quit, stopped going, and then, like a depressed person kicking Prozac, waited anxiously for the fallout. I stopped just shy of a month before the day my first big manuscript was due to my publisher, a memoir about growing up black and Jewish, and the culmination, in many ways, of all my years on the couch. The timing surprised me, but not my closest friends. They interrogated me at first, but then, convinced I wasn't avoiding some deeper, more horrid truth, offered their congratulations. I accepted their cheers, but inside I was incredulous. In my life successful therapy gave birth to successful writing, and successful writing reflected successful therapy, and that was how it was.

For the better part of ten years I had subjected myself—my motivations, fears, and desires—to a sharp scrutiny that bore fruit: insights, yes, but also articles, essays, and book proposals. In therapy I found for my work and process an ally, a cheerleader, the endlessly supportive parent I never had. I was no longer alone at the computer, at my desk, in my little room. Writing was still godawful and lonely, but never as unbearable as when I didn't have a sympathetic ear in which to agonize about the horrors of committing my thoughts to the page. It was a nice arrangement, but then one day everything changed. Inexplicably, I wanted to sit alone again, without a pep squad. I was shocked.

I started therapy, or *analysis* as Marie, my first therapist called it, my junior year in college. I was at Yale and, for the first time in my life, I was experiencing a discomfiting loss of control over my mind. Thirty or more times a day, while I was sitting in a crowded lecture hall, or a bustling restaurant, or while walking down a tree-lined street, an image of a huge and bloody ax formed in my mind, and, without any prodding from me, said ax proceeded to slice through a small and tender pair of breasts that looked curiously like my own. The sequence, which lasted no more than a few seconds and played in my mind just as graphically and smoothly as a film on a screen, ended with the bloody orbs, dripping and flaccid, lying lifeless on a slab of white Formica.

To talk about this phenomenon I commuted once a week from New Haven to Manhattan, relishing each moment of the journey. First the turning away from the imposing stone buildings of school, with its ringing clock bells and walk-lined squares, then the joining with my fellow travelers aboard the giant metal snake of Amtrak. For two hours I was mesmerized, staring serenely out the window as wheat-colored fields became tidy suburban enclaves, and as those morphed into dingy urban sprawl, and finally—blink!—the glittering metropolis emerged, as if all that came before was only the skin of the fruit, now peeled away to expose the real flesh inside.

After trudging through leaves and snow and rain, I arrived at Marie's decaying brownstone on the Upper West Side and rang her bell, a little black button encased in a wall of limestone. Within moments she either appeared with her typical masklike, utterly inscrutable expression, or buzzed me in, leaving our first encounter to the inner sanctum. Either way, once inside the Room, I always nattered awkwardly for a while about the weather, asked Marie about her day, and fired some baby talk at her dog (a fluffy white creature who spent the duration of our sessions lying asleep at her owner's feet).

Marie always responded laconically, and I took her terse replies as a sign that I should get on with the business at hand.

And so, after a few more fidgety moments on the white leather sofa, I poised myself at the brink, and dove into the swirling waters of my psychoemotional life. I fished and swam, swam and fished, until eventually I found my treasure and my stride, managing a tone and rhythm I only ever achieved, for her and with her, in that little room. Under her piercing, steely gray gaze, I talked about the young man I had fallen in love with the year before when traveling in Africa and how conflicted I was about marrying him as I had, for a few deluded months, planned to do. I talked about the cold masculinity of Yale, of my stern, disapproving professors, and my skeptical, competitive, and endlessly striving classmates. During some sessions I stared out through the thick and curling black iron bars on her window and said nothing, and during other sessions I cried, usually when Marie made some slight observation that made me feel heard, seen, and understood in a way I had longed for my whole life.

At this time in my life I wrote, but not too much and not very often. I had published a few pieces and had an intuitive knowing that I could write, that I had a natural affinity with the process of sitting down at the computer or the page and keeping up my end of the back-and-forth tapping between us. What I did not, ever, think about was writing itself—how did it work, where did it come from? Did I want writing to be my main job? What purpose did it serve in my life, and did it have anything to do with my breasts being chopped off?

At Marie's suggestion, I began to keep a journal more or less consistently, rather than in sporadic episodic bursts as I had since fifth grade, and to write down more of my dreams in an attempt to understand what was happening in my psyche. This proved a challenge for two reasons. The first was Kiswahili, a language requirement that ended up being the only early morning class of my whole college career and that, to my horror, met every morning at eight-thirty. Five times a week my alarm clock shocked me out of both my dream state and my ability to remember anything from it.

The second obstacle was my then boyfriend, who on weekends—my only remaining days for possible dreamwork—desired to jog at the crack of dawn and to chat as he prepared to do so, which drove me nuts. The moment I heard his voice my dreams turned mercurial, slipping cruelly through my fingers. As I lost image after image and was compelled to turn my attention to my boyfriend's clouded but beautiful face, my handwriting became loopy and unfocused. Instead of forming a sturdy barricade meant to keep the ax from hitting its mark, my sentences trailed, unfinished, off the page.

Deborah was my first unquestionably *successful* therapist, which means that not only did I figure out some important things about myself, but I wrote and actually finished pieces during the months and years that I met with her. Deborah was referred by a fellow writer, a self-identified black lesbian with whom I had become friendly and with whom, at the time, I shared both a publisher and an editor. She gave me Deborah's number after I confided to her my struggle to get going on the collection I had been signed up to edit, and the frustration I was feeling in my romantic relationship, my first with a woman.

I was also often finding myself bored during my sessions with Marie, and feeling stuck. While we had made several breakthroughs together—not the least of which being the discovery that the hand wielding the ax in my bloody fantasy was my own—I was tiring of the way I felt Marie withheld from me, the way she scribbled on her yellow pad more often than she offered a coherent thought, the way she nodded silently as I flailed about, and evaded my questions when I asked pointedly for advice. And there was something else. While I empathized with and connected to her Jewishness, and during our sessions was moved by the photographs hanging over my head of her mother and father—eastern European Jews who did not survive the Holocaust—I found myself avoiding the topic of race, or more specifically, of blackness. In her office I was far more comfortable discussing the Jewish side of my family, my father and stepmother and their two children, and my time in a mostly Jewish suburb of Westchester. The other part of my experience, the black, of-color part, fell into shadow.

In contrast, Deborah was an African-American divorcée who had had a husband but who might have been at least bisexual and maybe even gay, judging from her openness to and comfort with sexual differences. Unlike Marie, Deborah spoke openly and honestly about her own life, and this allowed an actual relationship to develop between us, the mere fact of which I found extremely healing. She was an artist who had become a therapist late in life, after spending twenty years as a nurse and a few before that as a sculptor. She had at least one daughter, and grandchildren. The room we shared for two hours every week was warm and filled with deep red fabrics and light woods, a beautiful rug with an intricate, oriental pattern, and several abstract prints.

It was Deborah who ferreted out the inextricable connection between my writing and my general feelings of self-esteem, Deborah who worked on the latter by gently pushing me to focus on the former. With her encouragement I secured a private writing space, first by renovating a room in my lover's brownstone apartment in Brooklyn, and then by renting my own floor-through in a different brownstone for an astronomical and completely unaffordable sum. This need to have a space of my own in which to write, a space I controlled and which wasn't prey to my lover's two dogs and three cats—or my lover herself, for that matter—was something I talked about on the couch for months. It was Deborah, not my threatened lover, who grew excited as I told her about my new carpet or the signing of my lease; it was Deborah who modeled for me the way my chosen mate *should* react.

Deborah was also persistent in reminding me of the progress I was making on my book, even as I moaned about how lazy I was and how I wasn't getting anywhere, and even as I asked again and again if a book on young women and men and feminism was worthwhile at all. I shut up when Deborah suggested that my feelings of inadequacy and pending failure sprang from a source other than absolute truth. And finally, after fighting every sentence, I finished the book.

I stopped seeing Deborah when my third, and I like to think last, therapist came into my life almost three years ago. Benito was referred by a friend who said that he worked fast and didn't muck around too much in the swamp of childhood. I had been thinking that maybe Deborah was too nurturing and empathetic, and wondering aloud what it might be like to work with a man. The transition wasn't smooth; when I started seeing Benito I felt a tremendous amount of guilt. He was an Italian who had converted to Judaism, a politically conscientious white man married to a prominent African-American woman. He reminded me of the father I felt I'd lost when my parents divorced, and as I gradually came to my decision to see him instead of Deborah, I relived ad nauseam my childhood anxiety about betraying one parent by choosing the other.

For the few months it took my conscience to catch up with my mind, Deborah and I played a kind of charade. I came to sessions with tales of my distrust of Benito, testing the waters to see if she needed or wanted to make him the evil outsider. I dragged out all of my nagging insecurities about him, while she calmly, patiently shot them all down and placed the responsibility of my decision to work with him squarely where it belonged: on *me*. If Deborah felt jealous she didn't let on, and she continued to give me the same loving support I craved, even though it ultimately enabled me to leave her.

After three years of rather dry analysis, and three of emotionally supportive and empathic psychotherapy, Benito's bracing confrontational style and intense intellectual rigor were like a blast of crisp, icy air. At the time we began to work together, I was entering into a promising though deeply troubled relationship with someone who was not only mentally ill but also in recovery from substance abuse. Not surprisingly, I had leaped into this relationship just weeks after signing my second book contract. Even though my new lover was just as committed as I to working toward a healthy relationship through regular, intensive therapy, the whole endeavor was a black hole of distraction—love being in my writer's mind at least as worthy of my time and energy as my book.

From almost the very beginning, Benito—perhaps because he was a writer himself—was optimistic about my capacity to be deeply committed to both my work and this new person. Deborah had raised her eyebrows and conveyed in hushed tones her opinion that it would be almost impossible for me to maintain my own life while in a relationship with someone with such tremendous needs; in contrast, Benito seemed to think that with the right tools the relationship could make me even stronger, more able to navigate the various pulls and pains of life, more able to achieve a balance between engagement and solitude, between Others and Self.

I sat somewhere in between. I hoped Benito was right, but I also couldn't deny that I hadn't written in months. Not only wasn't I writing, but I didn't *miss* writing: in fact, aside from my awareness of the book deadline looming overhead, it rarely crossed my mind. The more I reveled in the new intensity of my love, the less I felt the need to revel in myself, which meant that no fewer than six months passed without my having written a word. And then, during a plane ride across the country to meet my beloved, I started to get *very* antsy. In anguished tones on the phone, I exclaimed to Benito that I loved this person but how could I possibly do this thing, this draining intense relationship *and* write my book? Had Deborah been right? Could I not possibly do both?

Benito laughed at my torment, and then chided me for being overly dramatic and fatalistic. Yes, he said to my question, clearly, flatly, simply. Yes, you can have it all. And then, over months, he encouraged me to dwell more on the present than the past. While I wanted to draw a direct line from my childhood to the present, Benito wanted to help me make different, more self-interested choices *now*. He encouraged me to fight for what I wanted, to articulate my needs and have a hard bottom line—a process that was utterly foreign to me, but turned out to be as natural as rain once I got the hang of it. When I worried aloud that doing all of this boundary setting and emotional maturation stuff was great but that I still wasn't finished with my book, Benito didn't miss a beat. "You will be," he said. "You will be."

Even in the moments when I thought I was making a huge mistake and my literary career would pay the price, I felt in my gut that Benito was leading me in the right direction. When I followed his advice, I felt mature, grounded, and far less reactive than I ever had, and when he refused to indulge my lapses into regressive, pouty, narcissistic misery, I stopped indulging myself quite as often. With Benito's help, I consciously *chose* my complicated and intense situation, and came to understand and embrace it as a kind of developmental rite, a crucible, an initiation into adulthood. The result was that not only did I write many chapters of my book throughout the excruciating process, but the writing itself was, as Benito had assured me that it would be, richer, deeper, and more complex for my struggle.

Then something changed. Gradually, over a period of weeks, then months, I began to feel a little too comfortable, a little too embraced. I noticed I was restless and impatient while talking with Benito. I had so successfully internalized him, so completely integrated his unflagging encouragement into my life, that I felt as if I knew every word that was going to come from his mouth even before we started our session. I went over the same territory again and again, wanting secretly for Benito to cut me off, to recognize that I had arrived, that I was well enough, whatever that meant, to quit therapy.

At my desk I also started to notice an acute need to soothe myself, to turn and face the blank screen and whatever other terrors remained about telling my story without the added cushion of knowing Benito was a phone call away. I needed to sit in my study, in front of my computer, with no place else to go. I needed to choose my own work without anyone encouraging me or demonstrating the way.

When I did this finally, I found that I actually *wanted* to write. I wasn't terrified, mystified, lonely, or scared. I wasn't racked with my former self-doubt. I wasn't torn between my love for another and my love for myself. For the most part, all of that fell away, leaving me deliciously free to experience some of the joys of writing. The pure uninterrupted quiet. The magic of words falling into place. The experience of seeing another version of myself on the page, a little more than an extension, a little less than an alter ego.

The first few days after my last session, I constantly monitored my every emotion, scanning for psychological snafus I wouldn't be able to unravel alone. I had classic separation anxiety; I was edgy, sad, lonely, and second-guessing my decision at every turn. But a week later I felt fairly stable and slept through my usual session time with relish. Three weeks later I was writing up a storm and missing Benito not one iota. Two months in I realized that though I rarely thought about talking to him, I often invoked an observation he had made, or employed a strategy he suggested. Four months went by and I was missing him, not as a patient, but as a friend.

Yesterday morning Benito and I had a phone session. I called him because I felt, six months later, like I needed to check in. It was lovely. We went over the same stuff again and again. I felt the same impatience, which reminded me once more to get to work instead of to therapy, and which is how I came to be writing this piece. At the end of our talk, we said good-bye and I love you and I hung up the phone feeling lucky and proud. Lucky to have Benito in my life, and proud not to need him at all.

DOUGLAS BAUER

WORKING, OVER TIME

As was my habit, I pulled up in front of Dr. Mortenson's house at five minutes to nine. (And here's the sentence telling you that Mortenson is not his real name.) Before arriving, I'd stopped at the Starbucks three blocks down the street and eaten my morning scone while reading the sports pages—mundane sublimities that had become my ritual, four days out of five, for more than a year. Now, in the few minutes before my session, I would sit in the car and order my thoughts, then cross the street, mount Mortenson's front porch steps, and ring his doorbell at nine o'clock. You might gather that I'm concerned with punctuality. Actually, I am *overly* concerned with punctuality, but that's not the point I'm wanting to make and, as far as I can remember, the issue—*punctuality: still laudable or deeply anachronistic?*—never came up in my analysis.

The point I do want to make is that for reasons I recognize fully only in retrospect I had, over the months I'd been seeing Dr. Mortenson, come to think of my visits as my job, as my vocation, as that responsibility the working man considers, with more or less stylized complaint, to be his daily grind. In some sense I imagined my ringing of Dr. Mortenson's doorbell at nine A.M. as a wage earner's act of punching in. And I had fashioned around this illusion the morning rituals followed by the great majority of the gainfully employed as they hurried to their days: down a coffee, scarf a scone, glimpse the box scores, gotta run.

At the time I wasn't exactly conscious of any of this, but looking back I see that I embraced the idea, embraced it and, until nearly the end of my two years with Dr. Mortenson, needed it; that my casting of myself as reporting for work when I walked into his office and greeted him and his dog, Sophie (her real name)—an astoundingly wired and enthusiastic animal, the Roberto Benigni of mixed-breed terriers—that this notion helped me validate what I often felt was a luxury and even an indulgence.

And so it was in that frame of mind that I got out of my car on this bright spring morning and looked up to see the same two men who'd just spent several days painting the inside of my house spreading their drop cloths over Mortenson's front porch floor, their easy banter, in the early moments of their workday, having already settled into a soft and steady exchange.

Reflexively, I turned and started down the sidewalk away from the house. I knew they hadn't seen me and it was my idea that they might leave the porch for some reason, maybe go around back to their truck for more supplies, giving me an opening to hurry up the steps and disappear inside. I gave no thought to what would happen when I'd have to leave the house. That was someone else's problem.

After reaching the end of the block, I stalled a few moments more, then turned—it was almost nine and alas punctuality was now a factor—and when I started stealthily back up the walk I saw, against my hope, that the painters were still very much there. So I exhaled heavily and began to walk toward them, and as I did I pictured my stride becoming a weird swagger-shuffle, something I hoped would suggest the primitive confidence of a pneumatic drill operator, while in fact looking more like a tottering infant wearing a full diaper.

Up the steps, onto the porch, and a bold hello to the painters, as if to say, *Well, I'll be damned, look who's here!! The people you run into when you don't have your shotgun!! Ha-ha!!* But I couldn't hide my discomfort and as it happened neither could they, so after our greetings, which did not acknowledge the plainest fact that we were meeting on my psychiatrist's porch, we instead began, in a scramble to find familiar social ground, to negotiate when they could come back to paint two more rooms at my place.

When at last I got inside, Mortenson, a small round man with thinning white hair and a grand noble profile—I envisioned it on the face of a Roman coin—gave me his customary "Please come in," and when I'd lain down on the couch and adjusted myself, he said to me, "So. Any feelings about running into your painters just now?"

About the walk.

Years ago, a former lover of mine and I pulled up in front of a local garage in a small town in upstate New York and I got out to check on a tire being repaired. When I returned to the car, she looked at me with much amusement and said, "What's up with that walk?"

That's the first I was made aware of my linebacker shuffle and it's the only time I remember someone actually remarking on it, but it's apparently a thing I do—fall into a kind of ape-gait when I'm headed toward a place where physical labor is either occurring or implied. Garages. Plumbing supply shops. Men in utility company helmets peering down into a hole they've dug in front of my house.

It's symptomatic, this walk, of an old dilemma and one, among others, I was talking to Dr. Mortenson about a great deal: that on some essential level I've been uncomfortable with the fact that I do not make my living doing manual labor. That spending one's days making sentences is not really work and as a matter of fact is something less than manly and never mind Hemingway or Mailer or their like. Or, actually, *do* mind them. Look what *they* had to do—hunt lions or box Cesar Chavez on television or stab their wives or blow their brains out—in efforts to claim their manhoods.

One result of my discomfort has been the strong rejection of any vocabulary which speaks of writing as a mystical activity, that language describing the process as one in which the writer does little more than take dictation for the characters speaking to him in his head. I understand, I think, why writing might be thought of in this way. It's summoned purely from within. It comes from some fortuitous alignment of emotion and psyche that is as impalpable as it is powerful. We can't see or feel or smell or hear that place where it originates, yet the effort of it all is to offer up to the world transporting sensations of touch and smell and sound.

Still, I've dismissed the assertion that the process of writing is magical or spiritual, partly because I believe that if a writer surrenders to such terms it can more easily lead to a kind of legitimizing escape from the regular doing of it. *Hey, the muse didn't show today. What was I supposed to do?*

But I now recognize, two years after ending analysis, that part of my resistance to writing was historically connected to that deeper unease I've been speaking of, that there was no way I could insist writing was "work" if it were simply an exalted act of transcription.

If I'd had trouble justifying the writer's life, the contemplative life, then it follows that I might have created an even greater distortion in imagining analysis—an hour of ultimate contemplation—as my work (even if practiced while literally lying down on the job). And I see now that it was a pretense made easier by the fact that I had, before beginning with Mortenson, just finished a novel and was living through relatively fallow months, inevitable ones for me, when I am not yet ready to seriously launch myself again. I had planned it this way, knowing that I couldn't possibly devote myself *to* myself while I was still deep underground making my way through the lovely cave of a story.

Furthermore, in order to see Dr. Mortenson, I did have to leave the house each morning, climb into my car, and be somewhere at a certain hour; which is to say, I got to my appointments the way most people get to their jobs.

Mortenson and I were not exploring *how* I'd come to these feelings about what work meant. We didn't need to; that much was fairly obvious. I was raised on a grain farm in the Corn Belt Midwest and I learned early on that I was not much good at farming. From a young age, this put me at odds with my culture, an exile I've written about in essays and a book, once describing my embarrassment as a boy when spring weather came and I sat in the classroom, conspicuously pale, while most of my male classmates wore first-pink sunburns after their weekends in the fields helping their fathers get the ground ready for planting.

I've told of the time when, as an adult, I returned to my tiny home-town to write about it, and was one night asked by a man I'd gone to school with, when I thought I might get around to doing an honest day's work. So stung was I, and so insistent that he typified a thinking that had no appreciation for the "muscular work of writing prose," that I entirely lost sight of the fact that he himself ran a men's clothing store, for God's sake. Manual labor? *How are ya? That leisure suit there is twenty percent off?*

No, my conversations with Mortenson had not been devoted to locating the source of my feelings. But we were certainly wondering what I might *do* about them, so he was clearly delighted to witness my encounter with the painters on his porch. What a perfect scene from which to launch the day's discussion. (I should say here that the coincidence of running into the painters was not so great as it might seem. Mortenson himself had recommended them when I told him my wife and I needed some walls redone. But it never occurred to me that I might see them at his house. I mean, his porch had looked fine to me.)

A perfect scene, then, for his and my purposes. And as I'd gradually gotten to know him, I discovered that he was the perfect therapist for this aspect of what was troubling me.

Mortenson, whom I'd learned was roughly fifteen years my elder, was a man of courtly refinement. He was a lover of antique clocks and flower gardens and rare calligraphy and Greek mythology. There was a deep quietude in his style and his voice, not unusual among therapists and analysts, but in his case a manner that seemed unquestionably congenital.

He was not, then, someone you'd suspect had been raised on a remote West Texas cattle ranch and who had found his way out, and eventually to Harvard Medical School and the world, by getting first to Houston for his freshman year at Rice. So, impossible as it was for me ever to imagine myself at ease in a life of harvests and hog market prices, it was at least as difficult to picture Mortenson a rancher, with herds, and, more to the point, walking with his air of eccentric gentility into the local coffee shop at dawn to sit with his fellows and talk about feed.

I don't want to leave the impression that we were alike. I am not a man of particular refinement, courtly or otherwise. I care little for antiques, nothing for calligraphy, know scant mythology and, as for flower gardens, I simply admire the beauty of the ones my wife makes. Still, our backgrounds had a lot in common, down to the single sibling, a much younger brother, and once I'd learned all that I felt especially comfortable to think I had an empathetic ear.

And indeed I did, though I got few additional details about his childhood on the ranch. Nothing much beyond statements such as, "Mercifully, there was a library in town, which meant that there were books." When I tried, he would, in time-honored fashion, usually turn my questions back on me, inviting me to *imagine* how he spent his days, asking me what I *thought* he did in the way of chores. I never profited much from this transference strategy, though he urged me to try, because it never stopped seeming a cat-and-mouse game: *Here's something we could do: ask me anything about myself and I won't give you a direct answer.* Or maybe because when I attempted to see him atop a horse, it was too easy to change the picture to that of me atop a tractor and I knew integrally what that looked like—a boy working frantically to keep the plow in the goddamn furrow.

(I do have a strong hunch that Mortenson came away from his beginnings extremely frightened of snakes. Whenever I was remembering some scene of boyhood distress on the farm—say, entering the dark granary shed to scoop up a bucket of oats and hearing the rats' whisper-scuttle of retreat; or in the chicken coop, being pecked by a pissed-off hen when I reached into a cubbyhole to gather the eggs she was sitting on—no matter what the circumstances, he would murmur sympathetically and then say, "And then of course there were the snakes as well.")

What I said in answer to Mortenson's question about my meeting the painters on his porch was that, besides the awkwardness of confronting men who did *real* work, I felt I'd been exposed, in a way; that I'd been found out.

"*What* was exposed?" he asked.

"I guess," I said, after thinking for some moments, "I just imagined them seeing me as someone with problems serious enough to be coming to a shrink."

"So you think they *don't* have problems. Do you think a man who does physical labor wouldn't have any problems he'd like to talk about with someone like me?"

Here of course he'd caught the flip side, the full bias, of my attitude: if thinking wasn't real work, then men who did real work didn't think. And yet, when he asked me this, I instantly conjured a few men I'd known growing up, and the image of them lying on Mortenson's couch staring up at his beautiful golden-yellow ceiling was even less likely than one of me steering a combine down the mercilessly straight and endless-seeming rows of a life.

"Well, yes," Mortenson said, when I admitted to him my inability to imagine "Truck" Randall, the town blacksmith, lying on his couch and speaking of the abject dread of death he'd carried since the day as a child when he'd watched his old pet horse fail. "Yes, of course, that *is* the stereotype. Which the writer's imagination must supersede, must it not?"

When I left that day, the painters were not on the porch, having gone around back to their truck for supplies. At least that's where I imagined they'd gone.

A few months later, I was driving one morning down the narrow alley away from our house on my way to Mortenson's, only to see a truck blocking the way. This is of course a common occurrence in the city, and I pulled to a stop to wait for it to be moved. I could see three workers in the backyard of a house that was undergoing major renovation. They were carrying pieces of broken-up concrete from a pile behind the house and tossing them onto the bed of the truck. As you might imagine, these were large, large men and one of them was larger than that, a "huge (half-) nude brute" (to borrow from Don DeLillo) who lifted and carried and tossed chunks of cement with ease.

He glanced back, saw me waiting, and then, with the others, continued on, making two, three more short hard trips from pile to truck and back to pile.

When at last I honked, they all briefly lifted their heads and took me in as though someone had said to them, "Look. A tree." Finally, I leaned out the window and said—yes, I did—"I've gotta get to *work!*"

To which the enormous one replied, "Tough shit," and turned once more to his slab pile.

I lost it then, as I'm afraid I sometimes do, a moment when heat flushes up inside me and triggers a humming in my inner ears. So I leaned out the window again and shouted, "Hey. Fuck you!"

As I watched him start toward me, his body rocking slightly from side to side with each slow step—The Walk, performed as if he taught a master class in it—a great and unexpected serenity filled me. I have no idea why, but it's true, and I'd love to think it's how one feels at the moment of one's death. I simply sat there, watching through the windshield as he was approaching, and what I thought was: Well, I'll be damned, he's going to beat the shit out of me. I wonder how he'll do it? I wonder where he'll start? I wonder if I'll try to throw a punch or two myself? If I do, I have to keep my thumb *out*side my fist.

In other words I was, more than anything, *curious,* as if I were watching myself calmly from a distance while a kind of powerful anti-adrenaline flowed through me. I felt urgently receptive to letting it all come to me.

He got to the car and bent down and peered in. His look was almost a parody of menace, almost *too* contorted with rage. I said, "Please move your truck." He held his look without saying a word and

I can only believe that he was curious too, curious to see close up what the face of idiocy looked like.

I said, "I'm going to be late."

After a moment more, he slowly straightened, turned away from me, and lumbered back toward the truck. He got in, started it up, and pulled over enough to let me pass.

As I lay on Mortenson's couch relaying the episode, he surely heard in my voice the timbre of a boy's exhilaration at having not gotten caught. For that's essentially how I felt and, truth be told, my pleasure was immense. I had met the Hun on his terms and survived, which suggested to me that I could be a Hun too.

I explained the scene to Mortenson in some detail, making it clear I knew it was silly to feel so pumped up about it, but that after all I did have only two options. Either I waited meekly until they deigned to move the truck, the three of them glancing now and then at the wimp in the car. Either that or do what I'd done—lean out the window and shout, "Fuck you!"

When I'd finished, Mortenson chuckled, amused, and not condescendingly, by the extent to which I was myself amused, and then he began by wondering what I might do the next time I found myself in a similar situation. My impulse, after what I'd just described, was that the answer was obvious: shout "Fuck you!" again.

Mortenson said that of course it was good that I'd stood up for myself, but "wouldn't it have been better to get out of your car and walk over to the guy and say, 'I know it's a real inconvenience to have to park a truck in these narrow alleys, but I've really got to get by,' and if he still resisted, then you could say, 'Look, I'm not trying to give you a hard time, I'm not trying to be adversarial, but if you don't move it right now, you leave me no choice but to go in and call the cops.'

There was a pause and then he added, "That would seem, to me anyway, a somewhat surer way of handling it."

A more *adult* way of handling it.

That's really what Mortenson was saying, of course, and over the next several months of talking with him I began to glimpse the idea that that's what I would do well to become—an adult. And with this I began to understand as well that the moments of small shame I'd felt about my work over the years had a lot to do with a view that had gotten stalled somewhere in the mind of a ten-year-old who wants to be a heavy-equipment operator when he grows up. Especially if he's already learned that he doesn't want farming and farming doesn't want him.

So it was not that, as a writer, I'd not been a man. It's that, as a man, I'd not been an adult.

I wish I could summon a breakthrough session, a Joycean awakening, some one thing Mortenson said that provoked a grand wave of reckoning to wash over me. But we all know that life is not a tidy affair, that it's a stubbornly incremental narrative. And so, similarly, does the talking cure take its own sweet time, founded, we're assured, on the idea that it should.

Which doesn't mean there were no singular moments in my conversations with Mortenson. Plainly, there were—many, *very* many— and they tended to investigate the notion that we must all claim our rights, that we must all speak up for what we need and deserve, but that there are ways of going about this, when you're an adult, that are relatively less fraught, less emotionally perilous.

One day I said to him that I sometimes had the feeling I was moving through my days before an audience. That I sometimes felt so self-conscious it was as if I were performing, not living, my life. And he responded that this sounded to him like a child's motivations, the way a child behaves in anticipation of a judgment, utterly dependent on someone's approval and utterly fearful of reprimand.

One day I said to him that I couldn't understand why I so hated confrontation, and he said, as we talked about this, that children don't know the rules of the adult world, and rightly get the message that they are powerless to make them.

"I am an adult. I am an adult." There are moments now when I recite this, mantralike, to myself. And it helps. It even helps on the tennis court, especially when I'm about to serve, facing set point. I think, "I'm an adult," and I feel instantly more relaxed. Go figure. I have joked with Mortenson that this benefit alone was worth the time and money.

But not long ago, I recited it before picking up the phone to talk to a lawyer who represented the woman who was buying our house. There was an issue about two chandeliers we were taking with us and how much we were obliged to pay in compensation.

Quickly enough, the conversation grew contentious, and then the memory of the giant in the alley came to me. "Look," I said, "I'm not trying to be adversarial . . ."

It did me no good whatsoever, which only goes to prove the obvious. Why in God's name did I ever think that being able to reason with a man who lifts concrete means that engaging in similarly adult behavior will do you any good with a lawyer? Maybe it's evidence I've got a ways to go that, after I'd hung up, I very much wished I'd said to him, "Hey. Fuck you." Or maybe it's evidence that I've gone just far enough.

When I told Mortenson that I felt I was ready to terminate, he suggested we talk about it over the next month. So we did, and along the way he admitted to me that he wished I weren't quitting. I asked him why and he said, "You had a few things you wanted to examine, you dug a deep, narrow trench of exploration. And that's fine. It's just that when I begin an analysis with a patient, I want to achieve as wide an excavation as possible."

I didn't think, right then, how interesting a metaphor he'd chosen. And I can't help wondering if he meant it deliberately for me, or unconsciously for himself.

But then, of course, analysis *is* his work.

As for me, I've recognized that it was not my work, and that indeed it was a gift. And it was a luxury. But it was not an indulgence, and it was vital that I was ultimately able to feel the distinction.

What I said to Mortenson, among other things, when he asked me why I felt I was finished, was that I'd begun to think about a new novel and the ideas were pressing themselves for my attention, an attention I knew I couldn't give them adequately so long as I continued with him.

What I might have said to him was "I need to get back to work."

If, in my work, I were creating a character of a housepainter who cut against the stereotype, I could do worse than to imagine one who has worked as a chef in San Francisco and Boston, keeps an ambitious apiary, and sells his premium honey to the best gourmet markets in town, and who told my wife one day, a year or more after I'd run into him on Mortenson's front porch, that he was hoping to be able to make enough with his honey to quit painting altogether, since he much preferred the sensory world of food.

I've never spoken to him about that morning. Knowing him and myself a little better than I did then, I don't feel the need to.

The day he was telling my wife about his life, he was painting our kitchen. Some months earlier, he'd finished our living room walls. They're a beautiful golden yellow, Benjamin Moore 313, the color of the ceiling I looked up at, four days out of five, for two years.

THE REINTRODUCTION

OF COLOR

Stitch into your crimson dress a rose, a bowl, a code. Stitch into your beautiful dress a sentence of your own—a room into which one day you will walk.

—for Joan Einwohner

Once I roamed in blinding green. White punctuating the scene. Dandelions in August. Blow on them and they would disperse and scatter their seeds. Brilliant yellow flowering the next spring.

I was drenched in sunlight. Golden seemed to make a sound. The brilliant blue. Happy, dreaming, lilting child. Look at her, roaming as she is now toward her next adventure, in a place of complete wonder, iridescence. Poodles on a jumpsuit. Beside a blue lake watching the sunfish—and their young, just hatched. You could almost scoop them up in your hands.

Once red flared from the corner of her world: a beach ball, a bird in winter, the roses her father grew. She felt green, loved sage, the word *indigo,* a blue wave. A dock—that crystalline, floating feeling. Wildness of the child—her thousand enthusiasms. She tasted a red rose, petted the black swan that came to her, freed the fireflies her brother caught in a jar. Felt the terrible vibrations of the field against which that brother played. The child who loved the downbeat stepped out of time—hearing the world that way.

She loved being a horse perhaps most of all. She ran fast as the wind. A dark star blazed on her forehead. Running in clover, in heaths, o'er hill and vale—never mind it was suburban New Jersey, never mind. Limitation, like death, an unimaginable thing. Her heart beating wildly as she raced through every time and every terrain, *won't die, won't die,* her extraordinary tangle of mane, the nostrils flaring, the mouth and the eyes—devouring, the pounding of hoofs, universe, imagination on fire—the child.

Utterly dizzied by the contours of the world—and the word. Its rhythms—its heat and light. Of everything there is to say and everything there is to do and be. The pure erotics of childhood. The body's small but genuine heat—plowing through woods, hugging every tree. Dancing interpretive dances to the music of water in her polka-dotted bathing suit, rattling a pod of seeds. In the idyll that was her childhood. Her mother at her side, a more than willing accomplice. *Look, Mother, a baby bird has fallen from its nest, look, Mother, the rabbit's lair, look, Mother, oh look.*

The child wandered freely. Hers the tendency to joy, to pleasure, irreverence, kindness, empathy, dream. The irresistible universe. A secret, a private place.

She flew with arms extended once. She sang with fire. She dug in earth. Made perfume from roses. Dashed through water sprinkling brightly colored. Danced the can-can. Sang to summon the snow. Adored the rain. Made a May basket for her mother. Lined it with the most luxurious moss from her special spot in the forest. Listened hour after hour to music with her father. Begged the Virgin Mary to appear. Dressed like a butterfly. Streamers flying. Staged elaborate puppet shows. Collected ladybugs. Tasted the night, felt the cat's velvet, memorized the sky. The stars seemed to make a sound like singing. And in the day the sun rang like a bell.

She raced to the edge of the known world. In freedom she imagined being anything, going anywhere. Everything was possibility then. All option. And if teachers or other forces tried to quell her enthusiasms early on—well, they were easy enough to ignore. In a blue wave, a star, a prayer, a made-up song, the swirl of her mother's dress—and they were gone. Didn't they always want to reduce a complicated and terrible and terribly beautiful universe? If in those years there was someone trying to rein her in or take any of it, any of it away, she did not notice.

A dark rose. A bottomless black cistern in which she wept. Prayed her made-up prayer. Made potions. Cast spells. A life of charms.

Imagine the shock then of late adolescence when the charms seemed to desert her, when everything she loved seemed to be taken away. Having roamed freely and unencumbered, the voices out of nowhere started demanding in a kind of staggered unison and from every direction the same thing—*conform, conform.* The message was death. Abandon song, *conform.* Abandon reverence, *conform.* Surrender your freedom and all you love. Against nature, against intuition, *do something useful.*

How did she find herself suddenly estranged and at sea in an adulthood not of her own making? Exiled. For a time she must have tried to struggle against it—but like a butterfly pinned, trapped under glass, she felt her once lovely wings disintegrating as she pulled away from the pins.

The hairline cracks already beginning to show during *the college years.* The stresses of the reading list. The stress of wanting to know what to do. The burden of a talent completely unrealized, utterly nebulous, just a pressing feeling, nothing even close to words on a page yet, not really. And that strange counterforce coming from almost everywhere. The message—*leave that all behind*—before she ever embraced it, or tried—leave it behind. Discouragement from every side. Even before she'd ever really begun. Good-bye.

Who is that sniveling baby who feels so terribly sorry for herself?

After the buffer of college, where the struggle for the child's soul began in earnest, she stood smack up against the arrogance and demands of conventionality, its breezy assumptions.

And the request—to go quietly—don't make much of a fuss over it. A struggle of wills.

Having been raised to be an artist surely of *some sort,* even her mother now seemed to be defecting. "Your writing—something to do *on the side perhaps?*" She thought she was protecting her from heartache. Alas.

And what about a family?

I do not know.

As she went from one awful job in one awful law firm to another she knew she was not going to come true. She was in mourning for something that did not even exist yet. She didn't even know whether there was any real writing in her, but the denial of the chance—the negation of—her mother, her friends, the country of course—all indifferent at best. *Yes, but what have you written? Nothing, of course. Not much.*

Give up your childish notions, your silly daydreams. Hurry up, it's time. Conform, conform. Date. Marry. Work at a real job—not writing for Chrissakes—grow up.

Look at that woman, once the ecstatic child, who walks slowly but undeniably further and further, into her remoteness. Not so lonely—not so lonely there really.

A young person's struggle. She felt the terrible weight of convention on her and the arrogance of its demands. The methods were subtle ones, but the message was loud and clear—*give up your life for mine, step into line, hand it over now, and go quietly.*

Who is that woman who asks for one hopeful thing and tries (it's a little pitiful) to console herself, or erase herself with recklessness, with sex, with anything she—what in the world is she wishing? A kind of rage, a fast-moving inside, surfeit of electricity in her head. And after a while—a few weeks usually—she would sink back one more time into speechlessness, dug deep and snug, it's dark in there, *she is, look, she is unable to lift a finger from the bed, or form a word—unable to form a word—oh yes, you'll be a writer someday!* The world flat and drained of color—only shades of gray and then and then . . .

E. M. Cioran says, "The universe is a solitary space, and all its creatures do nothing but reinforce its solitude. In it, I have never met anyone, I have only stumbled across ghosts."

How to describe the place where the woman takes up residence?

She waves from the distance to the ones she loves, stranded now. Cut off. Frightened by the gap. How she still sometimes wanted to reach them, touch their faces, say their names, have a glass of wine with them perhaps. But the world was losing its vibrancy, its color, its feeling. She felt herself in a shroud of white. And how the sound seems muffled. And the snow—not possible to move through anymore. And the cold.

The remote hand holds the vestiges of the might-have-been—but forgetful, indifferent, or finally just too tired—you let it go of it—that last recognizable part of you—you let it go. And you forget finally, completely.

And she steps into numbness without much of a fight, without much of a fight after all. *Estrangement and distance become her, don't you think?*

Can't remember much anymore.

How to describe that white world where from time to time she might make small trips out into a terrible, animated rage, doing awful things, and then fall back into speechlessness, a sorrow so pervasive—*Is anyone there? Is anyone in there?* Doctors are saying, lovers are saying, friends are saying. Helen. Is anyone in there? Increasingly difficult to know.

Once she dreamed in brilliant green. . . . Wildness of the child. Audacity of the child. That passionate, vibrant place.

A writer? You think you are a writer? Even if you were it would be treated with dismissal (and you're no writer because, let's face it, a writer writes, does she not?) She hears the scoffing of the bourgeoisie, the trivializing, the diminishing, the belittling of all that mattered most to her, whenever she'd come out for a little foray into the 1980s.

It is well past time to mention her father in all of this. He was the only one as she moved toward adulthood who never asked or expected of her the typical, the conventional. Exerted no pressure. No will over her. The least patriarchal patriarch in the world. She should become an artist. Whatever that would mean. He had been a trumpet player—he had been an artist—and he had felt (though he never said it of course) every day the gravity of disobeying that thing. He had been a musician—but was now deprived of a sustainable art form (for how could a trumpet player with five children survive?). He had withdrawn from the world. In part it must have been why. The price had been high. He lived in ice. She felt she was going there to join him.

Daddy.

Once the original, wild, insistent self is lost—how difficult it is to retrieve.

They lie in the amorphous dark and listen to music.

Somewhere she must have, certainly she must have still longed for that thing—wanting to hear as she once did—perfectly through water.

The parts that got lost.

She was expected to follow the normative, to put away the world's strangeness, its silences, its dark, its mystery and melancholy, and fall into mindless, cheerful line—until the intensity of the strangeness, fear and awe, wonder and sadness and everything you felt in silence, in the depth of your being, the power, the oddness, the truest, most important, original part of you—the part you could least afford to lose—was lost, socialized, little by little, almost entirely away.

Male editors at major houses are saying, female editors who have embraced the whole nine yards are saying:

Exactly what you should write. If you want to get published at any rate. And exactly how. So that even one's creative life was prescribed. In order to be published you must . . . orders coming down as if from on high. Place a character in a conflict and then resolve. Get the reader's attention through blah, blah, blah. . . . Engraved on a kind of tablet. Serious fiction must. If you want to be reviewed. If you want to be taken seriously. If you want to publish with us. The threat or promise of publication keeping everyone in some useless line. Everyone is gray and sounds the same. All our beautiful plumage, gone, all our vivid color, drained away.

Even the book is a box.

Do not take even this. Even this away. The one hopeful place. Even the book.

How to imagine shedding convention then? As insidious as it was, as ingrained. As ubiquitous as its message, stultifying, oppressive. Coming from every direction at once. What a novel is—what a family is—what a woman's life is—what a life must be. Where was this voice coming from?—it seemed it came from everywhere and nowhere at the same time. An admonishing figure.

All the diminishment. Her pale white universe. Slipping into a white shift, against white skin, and the hair prematurely turning white—*don't go,* someone whispers, but she can't do anything else really. . . .

The thousand inappropriate ways one tried to get free back then.

When she left the white world—

The thousand less than perfect, oh yes, less than effective ways to try to wriggle free—or at least to forget awhile.

I went to therapy finally as the result of an ultimatum. Helen said *go or I will leave you.* She said *someone could help you.* She said. And I could not bear the idea of the world without her. She said. And because I loved her I said yes. Though she did not understand. Though I did not believe there was help for me. Though the very idea of therapy made me cringe—*all that talking*—I loved her. She said *we can't live like this anymore.*

She said severely depressed, sex addict, alcoholic, disoriented, out of control, she said. Suicidal. No. It would have taken far more engagement to have pulled off such a feat. Far more moral courage. Still it could happen perhaps—one liaison, one toxic narcotic cocktail away. I protested when she began the litany against me, but still I understood it as such: I was suffering, had been suffering a long time—in the time before real writing—when I was lost. A debilitating depression, a world hermetically sealed off, punctuated by episodes of high mania—sleeplessness, delusions, rage.

A string of sexual encounters. Did it not suggest I was still alive? *Get help.* She said.

Through the estrangement, through the isolation I could hear her—but muffled.

She said, *or I will leave.*

And that I had to go further and further, look for more and more lavish, excessive, intense experience, more dangerous, more thrilling, to prove—*to prove what?*

How had *she* gotten that way—that dangerously happy little girl, hour after hour, year after year, engrossed in her make-believe world. In love with the solitary place of her imagination.

She said. When the world was white and sorrow fell like snow, and nothing, nothing seemed familiar anymore.

And I said yes. Because my life had become utterly unrecognizable, not only to those who felt they knew or loved me, but also to myself.

And on a day where the whiteness lifted, if only slightly, stumbling through drifts and drifts of oblivion in my pale shift, I went.

With real misgiving, trepidation, dread even, a deep wariness. On an animated day I might have said how I detested psychobabble, how skeptical I was of the whole endeavor. How suspect I found much of Freud—all his nonsense on women, on dreams. How hopeless, how useless. How much more clever I believed myself to be than anyone I could possibly find to work with. I went because I was forced to. She said.

To the office in the apartment on the Upper West Side. I sat glumly across from her. *I don't know what to say.*

Where even to imagine beginning? All that would be reduced or left out. Or overemphasized, because language could best speak to certain things, but not others. My reverence for silence, and for what cannot ever be known or understood, made this therapy business a very dicey proposition indeed. The tendency to impose false shapes, the simplistic desire for the assignment of cause, one's hunger for why, one's need for motivation, then solution. The preconceptions, the generalizations, the summing up—all worrisome, worrisome. And the language—oh God—*dysfunctional* this and that, *empowerment issues, abandonment issues*—how awful. The one absolutely intolerable thing. The debasement of the language. I braced myself for the absolute worst.

Born in Paterson, New Jersey
The oldest of five children
Educated . . .

Have I mentioned my penchant for privacy, for solitude? *To be left alone.*

Who is that woman standing off to the side, so detached, so removed from herself, *narrating* the events of her life as if recounting another life altogether? Why is she so filled with caution, with reservation?

I was struggling against every stricture—familial, societal, artistic—it exhausts me now to think of it. And it was something more than this, too. Did I actually think that this very pleasant woman was ever going to be able to help me with any of this? Of course not.

That white world where I yearned to go forever. Never come back. *Why is she there at all?*

But I was hurting those around me including those I loved—there was the real problem. Was I hurting myself—not really—no, not intentionally. To break out of the habitual, the deadening—in expectation, in habit, in pattern—it seemed necessary to cause some violence, some harm to oneself. But not to others. I had been asked to go because of the damage I had done to others, and I went because I recognized that damage—and desired not to do that anymore. I wanted to be free, but not at any cost. To lose those I loved would be intolerable—my last connections to this world. And, of course, I was not free in the least.

I go, I suppose, because I am unwell mentally. I feel myself at twenty-six to be dying. In a stupor much of the time, with an impossible sadness—the grotesque, thudding afternoons, slow and dull, how to make them pass? Unable to speak, to rise, to move. For weeks and weeks sometimes.

And on other days, without middle ground, turned on a dime, without a break, I am so manic, so hyperactive and sick with it, so unable to focus, to sleep, to eat, filled with every delusion and plan; I am genius, utterly estranged, outside, writing such astounding works, and so quickly, *works of art,* only to find when I look back at them page after page of virtually straight lines. Impossible, obviously, to decipher.

I seduce everyone in sight. Without much feeling. Going to the next adventure in search of someone or something to hold back the dead feeling.

And the raining—what's that raining sound? Then snow, muffled. *Don't go.* Last bit of world. Last blue shadow. Take another lover then. Another beautiful cup of oblivion.

Week after week I wrestled with it—if only I could describe to you, dear woman, show you the contours of that world—drained of all color—where I lay entombed, buried in so many inherited traditions, assumptions, Dr. E., I can't breathe or move.

Most people live lives of desperate accommodation, I find. Overloved as a child, I did not have the need to be loved or to please. I just wanted to live on my own terms. Not so easy.

Even the book is a box in this world.

First inklings of the box, of the dimensions of the thing: its shallow sides, its heavy lid makes an awful thud—and the early attempts to resist—trouble early on in the refusal to assume the ordinary way of things: the prom, the driver's license, the National Honors Society— teenage rebellion? Yes, at the time it certainly looked that way. All the small refusals, the casual, seemingly casual, sloughing-off of the prescribed identities, of ways to behave.

Oldest sibling, but no role model—my sisters and brothers watch their oldest sister in dismay. And entering the working world, appalled by the tedium, the language—that bantering all day long, that horrendous small talk—and the way the language was abused, disrespected. I sat in mortal misery, suffering it, incapable of entering their various pacts.

Is she making sense? Is she making any sense?

The original self was slowly usurped. Without exactly noticing at first. It was just a hollow feeling, a feeling of something being slowly taken away, pulled gently from you as you watched, half cognizant but helpless. The wild self being normalized. How difficult to retrieve a life, once relinquished. One felt someone, somewhere, getting a sinister pleasure from this. The more you balked, the more exhausted you became. All part of the plan.

My parents next to me—people I desperately loved—and yet I could not follow. Their dreams and notions seemed to me not their own but things they had borrowed, a weird loan they had accepted without much question. I loved them, but could not love their assumptions. I would have to break their cherished, their given—not because I wanted to—but in order to survive. It sounds melodramatic, I know, but it was the terms of the struggle then. The struggle against those forces was the fight literally for one's life.

I sat across from her. *You are up to it,* she seemed to be saying. She gave me a taste for it. *Don't give up.*

And somehow not to fill that vacuum, that loss of coordinates, with cynicism, disengagement, withdrawal, self-protection, guilt, rage, sorrow. Somehow.

We sat there together and circled it week after week, year after year. Through the thousand retreats and reversals and dismissals and setbacks.

As I walk yet again into another darkened bedroom, another alleyway—*begin again.* Back to my bed. *Begin again.* And all the weeping. Then silence. *Again. Begin again.*

The struggle to freedom.

The struggle not to emerge already constructed.

To walk away from oppression in mind, spirit, and body, in full knowledge of the consequences. To live outside the usual tyrannies. To separate finally not from those one despises or is indifferent to— that is easy enough—but from the ones one most deeply loves—so as to be autonomous. To walk out of every enclosure. Fluent at last in one's own language. One felt often in that room the strictures of language, the strictures of all existing forms: literary, emotional, social, political.

> Put something down.
> Put something down some day.
> Put something down some day in my.
> In my hand.
> In my hand right.
> In my hand writing.
> Put something down some day in my hand writing.

Those lovely lines of Gertrude Stein.

I was unable to live within the expected perimeters, tired of the usual assignments. I am more lucid about this now than I was then, forgive me, I do not mean to reduce or trivialize, and I do wonder whether it is therapy after all that has made it possible to say these things: facile, useful, but perhaps not entirely true—or certainly not the entire truth.

I have been uneasy from the start about writing this essay. I am not a procrastinator and yet have put it off countless times. It troubles me. The danger of this kind of writing and of all writing to some degree is all too evident, all too present at every turn. And in some ways it resembles the dangers of therapy. What is this desire to become comprehensible to one's self? To net the escaping one, haul her in to dissect and understand and finally display. The temptation, the risk is to assign meaning and motive in an attempt *to feel a little bit better.* Not so amorphous, not so out there. To fix the elusive self. To invent a character for oneself—and a role to play. The "I" stabilized, fixed on the page now, feigning illumination. What violence do I do to myself and to language, and to the magic of those afternoons with her? What did I learn there? What happened in that room? One can well understand the trepidation in writing any of it. What do I change or give up or alter in ways I may not even be aware of? What will I say here in the attempt to communicate something?

How improbable that she met me in snow offering a bouquet of brilliant reds and greens and gold, an offer to return—

Was it possible?

Why not? she asked.

Her good sense. Her strange faith. Her practicality. It was a consolation like no other. Certain things could be done, could be controlled, demystified. When her colleague, a psychiatrist I had been sent to see, decided to seduce this seducer, seduce this basket case in the usual business-as-usual, garden-variety abuse of power way, she reports him, without hesitation, to the proper people. Her clear-thinking, straightforward sense of things. One could not help but be impressed. She acts swiftly and without fanfare. And that is it.

And how, and I do not know how exactly, that Upper West Side address over time became a saving thing—a place to go—a place to look forward to in the way I look forward to that which is extremely difficult, challenging and mysterious, and essentially impossible— what I mean is, the way I look forward to writing.

How did she reach me in time? The charm of this life. How did I find her? This one particular woman—who never uttered a word of psychobabble, who never pretended there were answers, who never displayed anything but kindness, intelligence, and care.

Her cat, her sullen teenage daughter, her nice husband, who would from time to time make an appearance—the magic of those afternoons in that prewar Upper West Side building—it was a weird bliss—even when I left frightened, or in tears.

Never known such respite.

What was happening to me?

Here is a crimson dress.

Yes?

And I stepped out of my white shift.

A memory, a pressure. Color—in a world bereft of color. Crimson. Vibration of blue. Touch of ocher. The beloved world—a slow coming-to.

I did not dare to hope. A memory of vibrancy. Step. Ascent. Motion. Memory of motion. Not dare. Memory of scent. Of collecting mosses in the forest. Plush. Green. Once she dreamed. Grace notes. Moments of grace. I did not dare. My father and I again in the moody Saturday afternoons listening to music. Every flower. Each and every. Blooming in the snow white of my mind's eye. Like a rose in winter opening.

Blue and red and gold brocade, stitch.

Streamers flying after.

Here is a wish, stitch.

What happened there?

Two women sitting together in a dark room on the Upper West Side of Manhattan on those days of bottomless agony when nothing seemed to give way.

We make a dress together. Something it might be possible to wear. And imagine somewhere it might be possible to live again.

There was safety there in that room with her, harbor, rest, comfort. Intimations of limitless possibility, integrity, pure health. Creating a place for one's deepest longings—a child perhaps, a piece of writing never seen before. The wanting comes back. All the hope. I scarcely can believe.

In that world completely drained of color, we choose red. Here is a thread.

Pass the black cotton through the needle's eye and watch. Be patient. Here is a silver fish, a star, a sequin, released on a red velvet sea, swim to it. A glass bead.

Two women in the perfection of the struggle to be alive. One guiding the other. One older, wiser. Here is a strand of gold.

To live outside the thousand impositions. To live one's life without inordinate fear, without needless apology. To invent oneself from scratch, if necessary. Here is a blue thread now.

Accretion of the afternoons, years. Time passes. Something happens. Impossible to describe or quite understand.

That opening. That clearing in the woods. A kind of hard-earned logic.

The incredible dimensions of her kindness and intelligence and discretion. Her compassion, her intuition, her open-mindedness. Utterly free of dogma or cant. The exact opposite of what the young woman expected, grimly waiting in that waiting area the first day.

Of what I expected.

To examine calmly all the destructiveness—and to look at it as if from a distance—and not judge.

When the world is snow, is flat, is cold, when all you want to do is to lie down and die into it—step into that dress.

Stitch all your wishes, fears, and the words you love most. Inscribe a hope, a worry, a sentence of your own.

Embroider your name someday. In your own handwriting.

Have I ever thanked him? I wonder. I think I have not. My father with his unconditional love and his unspoken but complete support. My silent, melancholy father, the only figure of genuine consolation—because he understood what the others could not—in this whole universe.

Yellow flowers—those were buttercups. *Do you like butter?*

Passing through a field of green.

Running through a field of green.

No epiphanies, no closure, just patterns, trends, a belief in the design. No reasons. No solutions, just the embracing of complexity, ambivalence, contradiction. No false crescendos. No answers. Only one's life *there, there*—stretched out before one—open again. Given back. Taken back. Those endless afternoons.

Blue and green and gold brocade. Feathers, bells, someday.

The motion was toward fearlessness—or less fear—toward stepping into one's very own life without concession.

The soul's journey toward small light—the struggle toward freedom. The same journey I continue on now, alone, as is necessary. As it must be.

I write every day—to be well. Have done it now for some time. Revel in it—the solace that comes from making shapes, the joy that comes from high seriousness, the humility I acquire at every turn from the impossibility of the task.

It was the reach in that room, Dr. E., that was so beautiful.

Is there any way I can ever let you know all that it meant to me?

How extraordinary to try and write oneself free. To live inside the language. The lifelong motion toward original expression. How very extraordinary a way to spend one's little time here. How very extraordinary.

I know I have never been ordinary—not even back then—as I called to my mother who I loved so much—*Mother, Mother*—it was as if from a great distance. I was always a little outside, even then. It might have been a clue.

Human voices—they come, they die away.

A few connections now—more than enough—Helen, my parents, a handful of friends . . .

And this. This luminous alphabet.

And oh how now the syllables move to round and soft, to coo and smooth. To safe. To dream. Look, how it is possible to invent one's life—on one's own terms—entirely--almost entirely. And I am happier than I have ever been—seven months pregnant now. How can I describe this state of grace? Having finally moved through another construction, another constraint, as if through water to the other side.

Blue and green and sparkling. This miraculous life.

It was the reach in that room that was so beautiful. It was the dream.

PHILLIP LOPATE

COUCH POTATO

My Life in Therapy

Like someone who is easy to hypnotize, I have always been a willing analysand. And a frequent one: I count ten psychotherapists consulted from age eighteen to my midfifties. You would think someone in treatment so often would have the deepest psychological problems—at the very least, manic depression or work dysfunction; but no, I am fairly even-tempered, rarely if ever depressed, and one of the most prolific writers I know. Rather, I regard therapy as an aid in life's situational crises, and, I suppose, as a treat I am entitled to give myself from time to time.

I must have gotten that sense of therapeutic entitlement from my parents. Though they had precious little money for "extras" such as therapy, trying to raise four children while working in the New York garment industry, first as factory workers, then as clerks, they were swept up in the postwar vogue for psychoanalysis, when even westerns (*Pursued*) and romantic mysteries (*Spellbound*) offered Freudian solutions. My mother, particularly, was enthusiastic about psychotherapy, as it gave her a godlike ally (Dr. Jonas of Grand Concourse, the Bronx) and an articulate vocabulary with which to voice her discontent with my stoic, passively resistant father. She even pressured him to see Dr. Jonas a few times; but my father, while intellectually friendly to psychology when he met it in books, clammed up on the couch. I was confident I would do better, and grew up looking forward to the day when I could tell my thoughts and troubles to a trained, sympathetic ear. (I should explain that I have always had the impression, rightly or wrongly, that I cannot make myself heard in my large, histrionic family, all of whom seem better at grabbing the floor. One result was that I became a writer, so as to have my uninterrupted say; the other, that I kept being drawn to psychotherapy.)

I was jealous when my older brother got sent, in high school, to a weekly shrink with the irresistible name of Magda, because his low grades did not jibe with his high I.Q. and because he made enemies easily. I, on the other hand, was a top student and determinedly popular, the elected president of my junior high school. In order to signal the onset of adolescent turmoil, I wrote a lurid poem called "I Hate It All" and showed it to my English teacher, indicating that professional attention was in order. She replied: "But you, Phillip—you're our most well-adjusted student."

It was not until sophomore year at Columbia College that I found a way to express the disjunction between my externally placid, functioning style and my inner chaos by trying to kill myself. I landed in the St. Luke's Hospital psych ward: there, for the first time, I got to talk to a psychiatrist. But I ended up lying to him, or at least masking my anguish: I was so frightened of being hospitalized indefinitely there that I consciously staged a "recovery," enacting sufficient optimism over the next two weeks to convince the authorities to release me. They did, on the proviso that I enter treatment.

In those years, in the milieu around Columbia, gestalt therapy was the rage. The writer Paul Goodman exerted a charismatic sway over some of my classmate friends; and Goodman, also a lay therapist, had written a book with Fritz Perls, founder of gestalt therapy, about this school of psychology. A Goodmanite upperclassman recommended that I be interviewed by Laura Perls, Fritz's wife, who often matched potential patients with appropriate therapists. Before meeting the august Mrs. Perls, I fantasized about intriguing her so much that she would take on my case herself. But in her actual presence, I was put off, or I should say, intimidated by her thick German accent and haute bourgeoise Upper West Side air of self-satisfaction. Nor was she exactly fascinated by me: I remember she concluded the session by telling me to read Rilke's *Letters to a Young Poet,* which I took as her way of saying I was a cliché—the green, novice writer that her European culture had long ago put into perspective. Actually, I was already a big fan of Rilke's *Malte Laurids Brigge,* but—maybe because of who recommended it—I could not bear his *Letters to a Young Poet;* they struck me at seventeen as insufferably patronizing and creepy. (I'm afraid I continue to find Rilke a bit creepy, for all his greatness.)

However mixed my reaction to Mrs. Perls, I accepted her assignment a week later to enter into treatment with a Dr. Eastman. In retrospect, what choice did I have? Entering his office, I got a shock. There were two therapists waiting: the elderly, kindly Dr. Eastman, and a younger, more aggressive-looking type, who was introduced as Dr. Bloomberg. They said that, if it was all right with me, they would conduct an experiment of having two therapists in the room treating one patient. The gestalt therapy movement was trying out this new technique with a few cases around the city, and I had been chosen as a suitable candidate.

Well! I felt flattered. Not only was I finally in therapy, but I was getting two for the price of one. It took me several weeks before I could work up the courage to ask them what about me, exactly, had seemed "suitable" for this seemingly indulgent deployment of psychological manpower. "Maybe it's because you have an 'amphitheater personality,' " said Dr. Bloomberg, with a twinkle in his eye. I could never figure out if I should take his answer seriously, or if it was tongue-in-cheek; but I had an image of addressing a whole auditorium of therapists, via megaphone. I often recalled this "amphitheater personality" diagnosis when encountering my impatience with the doldrums of couple intimacy, my desire for an audience larger than one.

We settled into a triangular dynamic that I quickly transposed to mirror my own family: Eastman became the permissive, withdrawn father; Bloomberg, the prodding, pugnacious older brother; and I, the younger son trying to play one against the other. It was Bloomberg who relished the playful aspects of dreamwork (in gestalt therapy, the dreamer is regarded as everyone and everything in his dream, and encouraged to role-play the different characters or props); it was Bloomberg who was also quick to puncture my defensive arrogance— a mockery I found I loved. Eastman sometimes became an audience for the two of us as we sparred. But his main virtue in my eyes was, from his perch of avuncular, tweedy, pipe-smoking normalcy, to vet the sanity or legitimacy of my statements, and, by finding them acceptable or at least recognizably human, to make me feel less geeky.

So well did I come to mimic normalcy under their tutelage, in fact, that I quickly went from being a suicidal outpatient to a big man on campus, living with an attractive coed whom I would marry in my senior year. I was sorry when Bloomberg moved away to Albuquerque, but I continued on in therapy with Dr. Eastman until, as the ostentatiously happily married young man, my own sense of self-problematic diminished, and the therapy gently petered out.

Before leaving that period, I want to mention the influence that Freud's writings had on me. Since I have never been good at mastering philosophical systems, this influence was almost purely literary, but it was a strong one for all that. I had taken a course in Nietzsche, Freud, and William James. I became infatuated with Nietzsche's sniping, truth-that-hurts, epigrammatic style, and saw Freud as Nietzsche's kindred spirit: more modulated, certainly more Jewish, but equally bracing in his courage to say the unpalatable, to entertain the intellectually perverse thought. Freud's freedom to analyze the causes of pain and suffering, his refusal to make nice, were balanced by an extraordinarily reader-friendly style, which took you by the hand, providing smooth directional transitions, anticipating objections and addressing them in time, and leavening all with a worldly irony. In his recognition of the persistently humiliating and ridiculous, I saw him as a comic writer, a descendant of Montaigne and Molière; in his positing of the chronic trap between desires and chances for fulfillment, he had a tragic vision. But above all, I was drawn to Freud's style, which Thomas Mann himself praised: his attractively honest, flexible persona on the page; his novella-like handling of suspense in the case histories—complete with subjective-narrator shadings; his very syntax, which consoled even as it demystified. Whatever doubts have been raised in recent decades about his intellectual biases or personal flaws, I continue to regard Freud as a great asker of important questions, and a brilliant prose writer.

The maturity that I believed I had assumed with my conjugal vows at twenty proved to be spurious. Five years later, the marriage was unraveling; I sought out Dr. Fischer, a therapist who had written an essay that intrigued me called "The Uses of Perversity." In this paper the author argued that it is sometimes better to frustrate a patient by giving him the opposite of what he expects to hear—by applying a Zen master's element of surprise to the therapy. The article had a dryly humorous tone which I relished, and which I kept hoping to see in our sessions, though it never quite manifested during several months' treatment. (Perhaps Dr. F.'s use of perversity, in my case, was not giving me the desired advertised demonstration of perversity!) Our lack of connection was not his fault, in any event. The real problem was that I had entered therapy ostensibly to try to save the marriage, when in truth I wanted it to fail.

Lajos Egri cautions in his book, *The Art of Dramatic Writing,* that the key to writing a successful play is to pick that moment in your character's life when he or she is at the ripe, crucial turning point—any other will result in a failed narrative. In the same way, there are times when the entry into therapy is doomed to failure, because one wants, say, freedom and confusion, not understanding.

I ran off to California, as seekers of youth culture, drugs, and sexual revolution did then, and found myself up against a much scarier emptiness. It was not long before I went knocking on the door of a highly recommended shrink in Marin County, whose name I no longer remember. He funneled me into his therapy group. There I learned to pummel a pillow with fists while howling at mother, wife, or anyone else who had stood in the way of my needs. I also learned to thwack the furniture or other group members with a Styrofoam sword to let out repressed aggression. Always the obliging analysand, I was willing to try any methods he suggested; but group therapy, or at least this particular variant, seemed to me more like an acting class than a talking cure. I have to admit that, on the nights when I expected to "perform," I went through an inner impatience during others' turns, much as an acting student getting ready to deliver a monologue for his peers might. It was fun seizing the group's attention with my latest story. Even when they criticized me for sounding too much like a book (i.e., speaking in syntactically complex East Coast phrases that seemed to lack primal spontaneity), I was pleased. Let them hate me, I thought; what do they know? In the end they took me into their bosoms, and the leader even recommended that I become a therapist. He said he would get me admitted into their Esalen training program. This prospect scared the daylights out of me, even as it tempted me for a day or so.

In the years that followed, I saw a number of writer-friends go back to school, earn a clinical degree, and set out a shingle. Most of them were far too crazy and self-absorbed to wish on any patient. Still, there are doubtless many parallels between writing and psychotherapy: the cultivation of observation and detachment, the attention to language and its subtexts, the necessity for empathy. In my case, I knew I lacked the *Sitzfleisch* to sit hour after hour listening to other people's problems. But I often wonder whether I would have made a good therapist. What I did become was a teacher. Even more than helping me with my writing, psychotherapy gave me important tools as a pedagogue. I learned, for instance, that the best thing to do in conference with a student was simply to listen and keep my mouth shut, offering an empathetic grunt. I also learned to monitor my gut responses to a student, checking for the unearned fondness or disgust triggered by physical appearance, tone of voice, or resemblance to someone I knew.

Finally, I learned to discount student crushes on me as an inevitable transference.

After a return to New York City, and several years' involvement in the writers-in-the-schools program, I was selected as project director at P.S. 75, on the Upper West Side of Manhattan. I was expected to train five apprentice writers and filmmakers to work in an elementary school setting, lead by my own teaching, guide the regular classroom teachers toward making their curricula more creative, and trouble-shoot among the principal, parents' association, teachers' union, and sponsoring arts organization. I was still in my late twenties, hardly a sage, yet I found myself in the position of having to act like one. The job's responsibilities required me to manifest a steady stream of wisdom, patience, and tact. Though I knew I could always fake it (as I had faked maturity upon getting married), I felt the need for someone to monitor me, keep me honest, much the way a fledgling therapist needs a supervising analyst to talk over his cases.

My first attempt to reenter psychotherapy misfired. I had been recommended to a Dr. Gross, who seemed more interested in listening to his stockbroker's tips between patients than to my problems. By now I knew enough about the chemistry between patient and doctor in psychotherapy to liken it to romance: if it doesn't feel right by the fourth or fifth session, it will never feel right, regardless whose fault it is. On the other hand, if patient and doctor click (and usually, though not always, a positive transference can be effected in the introductory session), they can work through any number of resistances that arise. With my next therapist, I clicked. George Romney was, despite his English-sounding name, a Cuban émigré, with wavy hair, a tendency to chubbiness, and a puckish smile, who smoked thin cigars. He had that cosmopolitan gusto I associate with educated Cubans whose childhood predated Castro: a tendency to be amused by appetites and psychological contradictions. This angle of amusement was the way I wanted to see life, and did, then, fairly regularly—most often in the company of another similarly inclined. Those therapists—or friends—

I got the most out of were the ones who had the best senses of humor. It was not just that I required an appreciative audience for my jokes (though that was part of it), or that I could only feel understood if the therapist was attuned to the wry nuances behind my linguistic choices. It was also that I needed someone to model equanimity for me.

One time, feeling guilty, or at least uneasy, that I had made him laugh, as though I were manipulating the therapy for superficial ends, I asked George why he seemed to find me so amusing. He replied: "Well, many of my patients are depressed alcoholics, so listening to you is like a tonic." It was characteristic of him to give me an honest, straightforward answer, rather than turn it back professionally into a question ("Why do you think I find you . . ."), and the devil take the hindmost.

George was a Jungian and heavily into Eastern religions, two counts that might have weighed against him in my (Freudian) book had I not already realized that chemistry with a therapist is more important than his theoretical orientation. As it happened, I learned much from his Buddhist sense of detachment: principally, to witness emotions as they passed through me, locating them as distinctly physiological sensations in the stomach, chest, bowels, without necessarily acting on them. In my teaching, for instance, I could reach the point of thinking, "How curious, I seem to be very angry at this person," while not actually exploding, but storing it for a later time when I could figure out why. I had always disliked it when people in psychotherapy acted badly, merely because they "felt" a certain way and assumed it was healthier to get it off their chests. I preferred George's method, to feel the full intensity of the emotion, while still deciding under what circumstances, or how much, to express it.

I was writing a lot of poetry at the time, and often a poem would be sparked by some riff that arose in therapy. For instance, I began telling George about an incident from my childhood, in which I craved a pair of blue pants and finally talked my mother into getting them, then didn't like them once they were mine. He kept laughing at the story, I kept furnishing more and more comic details, and when the session was over, I went home and wrote "The Blue Pants," one of my most successful poems.

In a psychotherapy of many years, it is hard to sum up the learning process, though sometimes a stray remark may affect you more than anything. So, when George commented to me, "If only you would apply one half the intelligence you use in your work life to your choice of women," it started a train of thought that lasted for years. Another time, I was attempting to disentangle the knots of my childhood and family dynamics for the thousandth time, when he said: "Usually I try to encourage patients to explore their family issues, but in your case, you've brooded about it so much that I would recommend you put a little distance between you and them." I don't know if this is what he had in mind, but a few years later I took a teaching job in Houston, which removed me several thousand miles from the family seat.

By that time, George had more or less "graduated" me. He told me that I had reached a plausible accommodation with my day-to-day problems, and that the main reason to continue the therapy with him was if I wanted to work on my "spiritual development." No way. I had already balked whenever he started drawing Jungian diagrams with "anima" and "animus" in different boxes, and I was not about to take up the mysteries of Ramakrishna and the dharma at whatever-I-paid-then an hour. When I left George and moved to Houston, I fully expected never to go back to therapy. It seemed to me that I knew who I was, for better or worse, and could live with my neurotic peculiarities. My only regret, therapywise, was that I had never been in traditional psychoanalysis, or had even been treated by an orthodox Freudian, since I continued to revere Freud as a cultural figure.

I knew I could never muster the money or time to undergo a strict five-day-a-week psychoanalysis: it was a status symbol beyond my income, similar to owning a yacht or a country home, therefore pointless to hanker after. Besides, I felt "talked out." That is, until I found myself in an excruciating romantic dilemma: for three years I had been dating a wonderfully loving, mature, smart, attractive woman named Terrell (just the kind of choice George had challenged me to make), who wanted to marry me, and whom I could neither bring myself to propose to nor break up with. She was perfect in many ways, but far too refined for me—a lady, and I was no gentleman. I asked my friend Max Apple, who had become my new model of maturity, for the phone number of his therapist, a strict Freudian named Dr. B.

It will already be clear to the sophisticated reader that something must have gone amiss with this therapy, for me to use an initial protecting the doctor's anonymity. Dr. B. offered me a choice between traditional psychoanalysis on the couch and once-a-week therapy, facing him. Frugally, I chose the latter.

Dr. B. was, as far as I could make out, completely humorless. He never smiled, he barely spoke, he listened. I am sure I might have appreciated his help more under other circumstances, or in earlier periods of my life, but this time I felt I needed a quick intervention to get me to act. The problem was not dissimilar to the one I had faced with Dr. Fischer, around the time of my first marriage: I had entered therapy under the pretense of making a good-faith effort to repair a relationship, when all I wanted was out.

What complicated the issue was that I knew Terrell would never do anything to give me cause to break up with her. Dr. B. would not coddle me by "supportively" approving my alibis for leaving Terrell, nor would he pressure me to stay in the relationship with her. He treated me with the dignity of an adult, by making me face the decision alone; in the end, I broke up with her. It was the hardest thing I ever did in my life. I broke up with Dr. B. as well, but that was not nearly so traumatic; and besides, by that time I had already decided to move back to New York.

A new start, a new marriage, ten years into middle age, the responsibilities of fatherhood, and a couple of therapists later, I am back in one-on-one therapy—this time with a woman named Barbara. She gives good practical advice, laughs at enough of my jokes; we get along well. I had once promised myself that if I were ever to go back into therapy in New York City, it would be with someone "brilliant," the author of impressive books, probably European, who would transform psychotherapy into an intellectual adventure. Barbara is bright enough, but she is not a Milan school theorist, not a Lacanian, not a figure in the *New York Review of Books* dinner party set. She is recognizably, sensitively human—someone who lives in my neighborhood, in fact, whom I occasionally bump into in the street as she window-shops. Who knows how many years I will end up seeing her? I no longer feel confident predicting that I will ever outgrow the need for therapy.

As for the influence of psychotherapy on my writing, I would say that it has confirmed and deepened tendencies already inside me. From adolescence on, I was attracted to the confessional mode in literature and, with it, the whole dynamic of confidingness, rationalization, unreliable narration, and self-aggrandizement versus self-disgust. I ate up Dostoevsky's *Notes from the Underground,* Ford Madox Ford's *The Good Soldier,* Gide's *The Immoralist* and his autobiographical writings, Saint Augustine's *Confessions,* Rousseau's *Confessions,* Svevo's *The Confessions of Zeno,* DeQuincey's *Confessions of an English Opium-Eater,* Celine's oeuvre, Henry Miller's, Kerouac's. . . . I eagerly read the work of the so-called "confessional poets," such as Berryman, Plath, Sexton, Lowell, and disagreed with their detractors who found something unclean about their self-revealing verse, just as, some decades later, I could not agree with critics who lambasted the memoir genre for being too narcissistically self-indulgent. It seems to me that if anything, what is wrong with many memoirs and autobiographical poems is that they are not confessional *enough.* They do not go far enough. I am endlessly interested in the wormy little thoughts and regrets and excuses that people have for their behavior. "Confessional" is a descriptive, not derogatory, term in my eyes. (My first novel was called *Confessions of Summer.*) It was inevitable that I should be drawn to the personal essay, the form with which I am now most identified, because of its conversational and confessional attributes. So, too, psychotherapy, which gives one the chance to confess and converse at the same time.

Honesty has been, for me, a literary lodestar, to which I never cease aspiring in print. I don't say I attain honesty, but that I try to reach it gives my writing a formal thrust. Similarly, I would never dream of lying to a therapist—what's the point? The therapy session gives you an ideal area in which to attempt to say the most truth you can. It offers the personal essayist concrete practice for the achievement of candor.

Having embarked on the effort to be as honest as possible on the page, I became more and more aware of the power of *resistance* (a term I consciously borrowed from clinical psychology). So, for instance, I might have been commissioned to write on such-and-such a theme (the Holocaust, say), and found myself dragging my feet, loath to express the pious sentiments I knew were expected of me. I began to employ resistance as an analytical tool, taking as a starting point my unwillingness to embrace the subject. I would seek out just those unpredictable, contrarian viewpoints in me that might give a fresher spin to the subject. The results were some of my most characteristic essays, such as "Against Joie de Vivre," "Resistance to the Holocaust," "Terror of Mentors."

I have continued to read Freud, Jung, Winnicott, Horney, Adler, Melanie Klein, Ferenczi, Reich, and more recent clinicians, as evocative species of analytical prose, much the same way I might read E. M. Cioran or Bachelard or Hannah Arendt. I regard them as my mentors and fellow lovers of paradox.

When I first began writing as a teenager, and my god was Dostoevsky, I came across a quote from him which said something like: "Why do they insist on calling me a psychologist? I'm a *realist*!" I remember, even then, thinking: "If I ever do succeed in becoming a writer, I wouldn't mind being called a psychologist." Every word I've written is steeped in, and dedicated to, a psychological perspective. Cultural historians are fond of speaking of the twentieth century as the era of Psychological Man; theorists of postmodernism talk about the coming of the postpsychological. Call me Psychological Man. French theorists who dispense with the individual self irk me. I want more, more, MORE psychological specificity!

In a *New York Post* interview I read as a teenager, Tennessee Williams said that he hesitated to go into psychoanalysis because he feared it would strip away the secrets of his unconscious or, at the very least, banalize their mystery. I remember worrying for about two seconds that the same would happen to me, before dismissing the prospect. What I must have glimpsed even then was that psychotherapy did not pose a danger to me because I would never be that kind of deep, volcanically subconscious Lawrencian writer. I stay close to the conscious, rational level, analyzing mental processes, emotions, and behaviors near the surface, conveying what I hope is a believable psychological map—whether I am writing or talking to a therapist.

NTOZAKE SHANGE

THE DARK ROOM

Long before I came to know myself as "Ntozake" or a writer, I wanted to be a psychiatrist. This no doubt had something to do with my parents' involvement with hospitals, sick people, poor black people, and me, following along to wards, living rooms, boardinghouses, examination rooms, and dark rooms where X rays were read or where violent, mentally disturbed folks were sequestered. My father, a surgeon, excised with delicacy what was malignant, diseased, out of tune with the body; my mother, as I understood it, helped individuals or families get in tune with society as a whole, to make living work *for* them as opposed to *against* them, without necessarily challenging the world as we know it. Both of these approaches left me wanting. What if what was wrong couldn't be seen or couldn't be excised? What if life as some soul knew it wasn't worth living without some violent catharsis? I credited Toussaint-Louverture and Dessalines, Tubman, and Anthony, with their simplified black-and-white depictions of living in our world with a pained, contorted mind and spirit. I was caught somewhere between the institution of slavery and the lost calls of the French Revolution. Surely there had to be someplace more peaceful than the E.R. or the settlement house. My ultimate answer was the analyst's couch, but before that I had to learn to live with my madness for a while longer.

As a child, I saw things. I was not delusional or schizophrenic, I could simply reach areas of my unconscious that others could not. The gift never left me, which turned out to be as much a burden as a blessing. I had visions. I wasn't playing. I was lying on the grass or up against a great tree, listening and seeing historical figures, artists, people I didn't know dancing with me, taking me to salons in Paris or road-houses in Alabama. I was daydreaming, I imagine, but I never relegated those episodes to anything less than my "real life." That's why journalists have such a hard time fact-checking stories on or about me. I will tell them an anecdote that is impossible to chart by any method. They may ask me if something happened, and I might say yes even if I only experienced it in my dreams, which I understand as being as authentic as my daily life. Before I started menstruating, this issue of truth was very much alive. What I believed or felt I could not always prove to anybody in a reasoned fashion. That's why I knew instinctively that I should not argue or debate because at a certain point I knew *my* truth was simply *mine,* and not a collectively recognized reality. Yet, it could not be a lie because I thought/felt it. The only place I knew where anybody else understood this was the psychiatrist's office.

That's why I dance. I can't always find the words to express my thoughts. I've come to believe there are no words as we know them for some things; but the body does have a grammar for these elusive constructs. They are not beyond articulation, but of another terrain. I'm becoming translingual so that I myself may speak this language. Maybe I was a passionate gopi girl at Krishna's feet, I don't know. I do know that my body extorts from me what hangs silent in the air. That's why psychopharmacology can only take me so far. I need my body to talk to me. My analyst watches all my gestures, both of mind and body; he listens as closely to my muscle burns and attitude turns as he does to my dreams.

Most of my characters have visions and dreams. Bessie Smith and Billie Holiday visit a character of mine named Sassafras. Indigo, another creation of mine, speaks with the spirits of the moon and the Ancestors. Lillane actually has an analyst. No, he's not *my* analyst, he's Lili's. Sean, the debonair photographer in *A Photograph: Lovers-in-Motion,* needed an analyst, but I didn't give him one. I let him suffer. He didn't have visions, couldn't talk to spirits or shoot the breeze with his own myths. His memory weighed on him too heavily. Is it the same for me? Not in the material world. But living with my being, I know now that if I *know* about it, it happened to me, belongs to me now. I was not present during the French Revolution, but I can describe Marat's bath and exude Charlotte Corday's rage and naiveté. Was I conscious at that time? No. But can I discuss it now? Yes. Without heart palpitations? Yes. Without clammy palms? Yes. Without blinking an eye? No.

When my work titled *For Colored Girls . . .* was at the height of its controversy and popularity, I found myself wearing very dark glasses and large hats so that folks wouldn't recognize me. I couldn't ride elevators up or down. If someone figured out who I was, I would calmly state that I was frequently mistaken for her. I'd had other occasions in my life—like when I was the only African American in a class or had been banished to the countryside that my family loved so much—when I'd been known to dissociate, to refer to myself in the third person. Then, I was Paulette; now, Ntozake is repeating the pattern of the girl I've gleefully left behind. But this transition was very troubling. I was in the frenzied act of disappearing myself. Now, I admit to discovering many, many roads to oblivion, but I rarely recounted these episodes with warmth or a sense of well-being. So I did what I thought souled writers did: I went to my producer, Joseph Papp, to seek counsel. To my alarm, Joe recommended *against* analysis or other therapies, "because then my writers can't write anymore." Well, writing I was;

living I was not. I wasn't always a strong supporter of my own perceptions. The ability to write in isolation for hours about anything and enjoy it is a gift, but it is not life. Even *I* knew this. I could not hide in a dance studio, either. My presence was unavoidable, yet unbearable.

Off to find a shrink I went. I was looking for a wizard, some magic, some chant or breath that might make being me something to look forward to in the morning. I have the capacity to sleep for four days at a time, if I am so inclined. At one point, I refused to get up and live my life among the living because my dreamlife was so much more interesting. But a wizard I did not find. I *did* discover that finding the right shrink/analyst is as important a decision as finding a soul mate. I've been involved with over seven mental healthcare workers in the last twenty years. The overwhelming part of that time was spent with three—one psychiatrist and two analysts. I lost one analyst to the emergency room. Four years of quasi-sane mourning passed before I was able to seek out the next, with whom I have been working for nearly a decade. With his help and astounding patience, I have lost my title as "the angriest patient ever encountered during all my years of practice," and have become instead the 1991–93 Heavyweight Poetry Champion of the World—as you see, a much healthier management of my violent proclivities. In all seriousness, I've finally learned to feel what I see. What I've been blessed to conjure in words is no longer two steps removed; my body is not a hindrance to my spirit, but a manifestation of it. I am still crazy, but not so afraid of that part of me. I can even tell jokes to my crazy person and realize that these are some of my saner moments.

To get to this point, I've dressed up as one of the girls who stole all the basketball players at my high school, just to prove that I *could* be one of them. That was a session to remember. I've felt what I'd swear to be electricity in my body. I've known the ocean and intense heat. All this actually happened while I was on the couch. Talk about terrified! Try being the Atlantic Ocean all by yourself in an eight-by-twelve room with ancient fertility statues placed like buoys all around. To this day, I don't know all I was seeing and feeling in that room. I've spoken in tongues. Some sessions I've only spoken Spanish, or a mixture of French and Portuguese. I don't know why; I only know that sometimes a foreign language is all that will come out. Sometimes I sleep. Other times, Paulette speaks. Her voice is different from Ntozake's. Sometimes I want to knock Paulette out, but since we can only use language as a tool or weapon or doll or whatever I need, I learned at least to talk to her; that is, if I am not wildly gesticulating in some recollection of a dream: legs flying, arms of a flamenco dancer, long Balanchine neck. I could never actualize outside my "dark room" where things, me, memories float out of syllables and become benign or empowering, as they must because they are never without meaning.

All of this is very precious. I must keep my eye on my different selves. I've learned this through a yearly, hour by hour, disciplined manner. It has not been easy. I have not been happy. I am not always careful. It costs a lot. What do I get in the end? Do I get better? How will I know when I get there? I could get coy, answer that Beckett knew what detained Godot, but we don't know that. I know I don't know that. Anyway, I have had a hard time explicating *le texte*. The characters never die. The stories never end for me. That's why I go unravel my loose ends with my psychoanalyst. Nothing is wrong. No one else knows. A pin could drop, but usually what's falling away is not so piercing, not so singular; it's the shreds of life I must make space for somewhere in myself. Myself, who is more than just "the writer," and therefore cannot continue to look for herself solely on blank pages.

Joe Papp—my "Art Daddy," as I called him—was wrong about one thing: psychoanalysis has made me a finer writer, a fuller person and a funnier one, to be sure. I've found beauty in characters I would otherwise have shunned. I've been able to take on the persona of someone puzzling to me, with no need for trepidation, and even with a magic I thought I could only pick up somewhere in the night. My analyst is Anthony Molino. He's a poet. He lives in Italy and, like a guardian spirit, with me.

One of Simon Bolívar's houses was hexagonal, seated on a cliff in such a way that from any point, he could feel/see land and peoples who would be free. When I lie nestled on the couch in the room of no color and all colors, I am in that house. I am on that cliff. I am one of those people.

MEG WOLITZER

SITTING UP AND
LYING DOWN

Nine years ago, when several of my friends were starting to take pioneering drugs such as Prozac and Paxil, and others were engaged in once-a-week, sitting-up psychotherapy with kind, attentive therapists whose walls held framed pastels and posters from Galerie Maeght, and whose words of advice were often as soothing as soup, I decided to enter traditional psychoanalysis.

I had been in therapy a couple of times in my life, and had benefited, to a certain degree, from those experiences. The last therapist I'd seen was somewhat unconventional, with a background that included a mixture of Freud, Jung, gestalt, and something motherly and indefinable. Her patients—who included several of my friends—called her by her first name, Carol. There was an informality to the sessions, which were held in her big, ramshackle apartment. Occasionally, one of her children would march through the waiting room, schoolbag swinging, or else a cat would slither past me into the office as I was admitted, and I would spend much of the session awkwardly petting this fat, ancient Persian that had climbed onto the couch and fallen asleep in my lap. Sometimes, before my session began, I could hear peals of laughter emanating from Carol's office, as though therapist and patient were actually having fun in there, swapping jokes like two old, comfortable friends. Her waiting room took on the quality of an informal cocktail party; often I would run into someone I knew and we would chat for a second, one taking off a coat, the other putting one on.

At the beginning of the session each week with Carol, I usually felt the need to provide a recap of the various germane things that had happened to me since I had seen her last. "Well," I would begin, trying to unscroll the entire week in my mind as I sat across from her in her sunny, plant-filled office, "I was pretty depressed on Thursday, I seem to remember, though it was so many days ago that now I'm not exactly sure why."

"Oh?" she would say, waiting for me to go on.

Then I would finally remember what had happened on that long-ago Thursday, and would launch into the story, along with a catalog of complaints, incidents, small slights, and piquant anecdotes. Sometimes we would laugh together, but mostly our sessions were earnest and serious and fairly melancholy. Tissues were offered, along with sympathetic nods, and bits of direct advice were often dispensed. At the time, I was pleased that Carol would actually give me her opinions and provide specific suggestions. It was a relief to feel that there was a reliable person to whom I could tell my problems, and who in exchange would help me figure out what to do about them. As a result, I was certainly helped by Carol on a week-to-week basis. Between sessions I often felt as though I were roaring and crashing and moving through my life as jerkily as a bumper car at an amusement park, but when I saw her on Tuesday afternoons at 2:50 I would let the bumper car idle a little. We would talk, and she was calm and consoling. And yet, and yet. I stopped seeing Carol for reasons that I can't really remember. We didn't *terminate*, exactly. We ended the sessions, more or less, because I was too busy for them. Whether I was sad or regretful about not continuing to see her, I can't recall. She got me through much of a year or so of my midtwenties, a time when I and most of my friends felt we needed a Sherpa to guide us along and carry our belongings. She was a reliable guide and not too expensive, and her comments and advice were practical and thoughtful.

It's been fifteen years since I've seen Carol, and in the rare moments when I think of her, I'm reminded of certain sexual relationships people have in their twenties, in which the other person occupies a vague, blurry role. The breakup, when it inevitably occurs, is never a traumatic rupture, but rather is characterized by a mutual drifting movement in two different directions. Within a few months, you can barely remember how the other person looked, or what you two spoke of when you were together.

Several years after I had stopped seeing Carol, I was about to get married, and for reasons that I didn't understand at the time, the idea of permanence—of actually belonging to someone—was troubling to me. I wished that I had a person to discuss these feelings with, someone other than my future husband or my cluster of friends who regaled me with their own stories of marital ambivalence and how it was all neatly resolved at the altar, or was perhaps never resolved at all. Briefly, I considered returning to Carol. I imagined my monologues about commitment and fidelity and sexuality, and her responses to what I said, but even thinking about such exchanges bored me terribly, as though they were part of a long and poorly subtitled movie that I was seeing for the second or third time. Oddly, even though I didn't feel that I wanted to be in therapy again, I knew that if I was to begin treatment it would probably have to be more than once a week. I sometimes fantasized about a Brian Wilson deal, in which the therapist actually goes everywhere with you, dispensing help whenever you need it, never leaving your side, even co-producing your latest album. I wasn't sure why I felt this way. I was not deeply, perilously troubled; I was not secretly cutting notches into my arms like the girls I saw on 20/20; I was not in danger of falling apart. I could function quite well, despite the bouts of anxiety that sometimes gathered like small, efficient *tsunamis,* then drifted away.

Around this time a good friend of mine, a journalist, entered traditional psychoanalysis. She went to a well-known analyst four times a week and lay on his couch while he sat near her head, mostly in silence. This seemed at the time, and still does seem, a peculiar, anachronistic situation, as though my friend were a neurasthenic woman in Vienna at the turn of the century. It is unnecessary for me to explore here the widely held notion that psychoanalysis is a thing of the past, an antique whose tenets are still occasionally taught in college psychology courses, but whose practice seems relegated to a few dusty, Persian-carpeted offices scattered throughout the major metropolises of our country, bypassing small towns and rural areas entirely.

Despite its decline, I seem to keep meeting people who are currently undergoing psychoanalysis, or who have recently finished doing so. When they speak of their experiences, their eyes tend to take on a certain devotee's light. They know they're in a minority, members of a group as dwindling as Shakers or readers of the *Daily Forward,* yet they've clearly been enhanced and changed by their experiences, despite the skepticism that encircles them. My friend, too, was not unaware of the near-absurdity of the psychoanalytic experience. The long silences, the demanding time requirements, the fees, the idea of lying down in a room while a stranger sits up nearby—it all seemed crazy to her, but still she went along with it. I was always fascinated to hear her stories. Her transference feelings for her analyst were strong, to say the least. She loved this elderly man, she dreamed about him constantly. (In one dream he revealed to her that he was really supermodel Christie Brinkley.) Occasionally, she even called his answering machine at night just to hear his dully recorded voice. A highly respected writer and thinker, she became punchy and almost pubescent when it came to him. Her analysand side was one step away from making "Prince Albert in a can" prank phone calls to her doctor. What was it, I wondered, that could make such a smart, sophisticated person suddenly become so dependent and besotted? It was as though she were a biographer who had quickly switched from writing a critical study of Hannah Arendt to writing about the Backstreet Boys.

While I found her reactions touching and perplexing, there was something in the fact that my usually formidable friend had been reduced to this state that hinted at the potentially transformative power of psychoanalysis. I did not want to be transformed to that regressed, babbling state, God knows—and I wasn't at all sure I would be, for all transferences are different—but I did respond to the idea of transformation. As my friend revealed more to me about her experiences, I saw that she seemed to have greater access to the actual process of her thoughts, the various pathways they took. This was evident not only in our conversations but also in her journalism, which had grown richer and more interesting, though I couldn't be sure that it had anything to do with her analysis. I was both impressed and wary, and when I asked her if she would have her analyst recommend someone for me to see, I was not at all sure why I was asking or what I would be signing up for.

The first day I lay down in the office of Dr. V., the couch seemed to tilt like a cradle, in danger of depositing me at the feet of this woman I had recently met and who had agreed to see me four times a week for an extremely low fee. I was unprepared for this strong reaction; I had imagined that the experience would be like therapy, only inflated and constant. But analysis turned out to be a territory that bore little resemblance to what I'd experienced once a week in the calm confines of Carol's office. It was infinitely stranger and deeper, not to mention easier to mock and harder to either justify or forget.

Dr. V. was a well-dressed woman of indeterminate age: younger than my mother but older than me. She had large glasses, wore scarves, and had a slightly weak, formal handshake; the idea of calling her by her first name seemed all wrong. It was as though I wanted to invest her with a certain kind of authority that Carol had never had over me. The idea of entering analysis with a peer would have been absurd; I needed someone both to look up to and adequately resent. Dr. V. reminded me of an art history professor I'd had in college; I could almost imagine my analyst standing at a great distance in a dim room, clicking a slide projector to the next frame and murmuring vaguely about the woodcuts of Dürer.

I dutifully began to give Dr. V. my "story" in those first weeks, the collection of details that I had always carried around with a certain kind of pride and wincing shame. Having to tell even one more person my old saws—about the argument between my parents during the trip to France, or the kiss-and-grope games played behind the steps across the street from my grandparents' building in Brooklyn when I was eleven—was excruciating and tedious, but still I slogged on. She would occasionally ask a question that would send me into further detail, until soon it seemed as though I had said everything there was to say. By then, I hated the sound of my own voice; if I had been an outsider listening in, it would have sounded like the teacher's drone in the old *Peanuts* TV specials: a nasal "wah wah" bleat that no one would ever want to hear.

Yet Dr. V. did want to hear. I showed up day after day, suffused with embarrassment at my own paltry stories and feeling a peculiar dizziness sweep over me as I talked. The room seemed overheated, and she seemed to be sitting too close to the couch for comfort. Our interaction unnerved me in the beginning, seemed perverse and odd and laughable; after a while, though, I grew used to the strangeness, and came to miss it during vacations or when I had to skip a session. The couch stopped tilting. I would almost never come in and tell Dr. V. a sequence of events that had taken place since the last time I had seen her, even if a weekend had passed. Instead, I would come in and start up where we had left off, speaking in the shorthand that develops between a patient and analyst. Sometimes I would recount the dreams I had at night that were becoming more and more peculiar with time, often directly involving her. Once, after she had left me a message on my answering machine about a change in appointment, my future husband picked up the message and gave it to me. "She sounded like she had a Southern accent," he said. "In fact, she sort of sounded like she might be black." Dr. V. wasn't black, but after that little exchange

I began having dreams in which a black woman would appear, and whenever that happened I knew she was a stand-in for my analyst. The dreams about the black woman continued throughout the years of my analysis, and sometimes I even had dreams about the opposite of a black woman—a very blond, nearly albino-looking woman who, in her extreme whiteness, was also a reverse stand-in for my analyst. In truth, Dr. V. was everywhere, sitting near my head four days a week, and inside it the rest of the time. She never said much; she rarely offered suggestions or concrete advice as Carol had done, but somehow she was having an extreme effect on me.

This was called a transference. It meant that the analysis was working. But it didn't, as far as I could see, mean it was *helping*. How were my feelings about marriage being sorted out by dreaming about black and white women? How, in fact, was I being helped by my relationship with this quiet, formal, unknown woman who sat beside me like a slightly distant mother putting a child to sleep? There were times when I almost did fall asleep, for the room was hot and the one-sided conversation was lulling. But mostly I stayed wide awake, and one by one I sorted through my various troubling feelings.

I got married fairly early into the analysis, but I stayed on afterward and began to talk about other matters. Being in analysis proved very useful in terms of my writing, and I spent many hours talking about a problem in a piece of work, or reading aloud a passage that I couldn't fix. It's not that Dr. V. ever said anything like "Yes, I agree that the passage is weak. You need to state the theme more clearly and use fewer similes." She said very little, but just kept quietly interpreting, translating everything that I said and sending it back to me in a slightly altered form.

My analysis bears very little resemblance to regular, once-a-week therapy, and shouldn't be compared to it. Though some once-a-week therapy is also psychoanalytic, and the therapist's responses might be similar to Dr. V.'s, the amount of time that analyst and patient spend together renders an analysis unique. I know that my analysis wouldn't stand up to psychoanalytical skeptics, who have proliferated wildly over the last decade, but I don't really care. At times I partially agree with the nonbelievers; psychoanalysis is, of course, unscientific, and it can also seem ridiculous. When I think of myself lying down on that couch, I am horrified that I've thrown so much money and time at this peculiar, baffling, ineffable enterprise. But mostly I feel grateful that I stumbled into that room all those years ago, and I know that because of it there is a different person about to stumble out.

GEORGE PLIMPTON

A SLIGHT ENCOUNTER

I have only had a nodding acquaintance with psychiatrists—coming from a family for whom the word "shrink" meant only what happens to wet socks. "Mother, I'm going to see a shrink" would be thought of as an odd misuse of language.

When I was at college, however, I became involved in a rather sophomoric "breaking and entering" incident, and because my parents were worried this might become a pattern, they suggested that I should "see someone." They used the euphemism "someone," since the very word "psychiatrist" suggested to them that their son was doomed, truly unhinged, jabbering, and was poised on the doorstep of a mental institution. My mother told me years later that they didn't have any psychiatrists in her day.

The "someone" they found was a Mr. Wooster who lived on Marlborough Street in Boston. I don't know that he was a registered doctor because I never heard anyone refer to him as such. He was better known as a counselor, his trick of the trade to instill confidence in his patients, giving them "a leg up" as it were. I became very fond of him. He played the saxophone, quite loudly and sonorously, and I would hear it as I walked up Marlborough Street to the brownstone where he lived on the second floor. As I walked up the stairs, the saxophone became quite deafening. When he put it away, we would sit and talk. There was nothing Freudian or Jungian in his approach. He knew that I had ideas about being a writer. I began to think of him as an editor—our sessions mostly taken up with his suggestions as to what I should write. One of his notions, I recall, was that I should do some research on the biological horrors of the South Pacific (the year was 1944 and our troops were island-hopping toward Japan)—poisonous insects, slugs, snails, snakes, and so on. "It's pure *Reader's Digest* stuff," he said.

He helped get me a job at the now defunct *Boston Herald*. I didn't write about the horrors of the South Pacific, but a story I wrote about Harvard professors eating horse meat at the faculty club made the front page.

Mr. Wooster loved the social life. I took him to some parties in Cambridge. At one of them he had too much to drink and fell asleep under the hostess's bed upstairs. I looked for him at the end of the party and assumed he'd left for Boston on his own.

She called me the next day. Her voice sounded strained. She said she had been awakened at three in the morning by the sound of deep snoring under her bed. She sat up abruptly, shouted loudly, and this man crawled out.

"Your friend," she said. "He frightened the bejabbers out of me."

"He did what?"

"He scared me half to death. My God, this *breathing* under my bed."

"I can imagine," I said.

"Well, who is this friend of yours?"

"My psychiatrist," I said.

I went into the army about that time. I thought of Mr. Wooster on occasion. He had a country house on Cape Ann, as I recall, where he kept sea lions, a pair of them, in a huge freshwater quarry. He rang a little bell under the surface of the water and they would come to feed from his hand at astonishing speeds from the opposite end of the quarry, roiling up waves as their heads emerged close by. I swam with them a few times, feeling the push of water against my body as they swept by, but not too often, since the water was so cold.

Not so long ago, asked to adjust better to a new marriage, I went to see a psychiatrist (still unable to use the word "shrink") for a few months, once a week, bicycling to his office on the Upper East Side. I have heard it said that psychiatrists' waiting rooms are uniformly dreary, rarely a window to the outside, or if so, facing the bricks of a wall a few feet away . . . all this designed to put the patient in an increasingly morose mood, the better to get him or her to spill the beans. My man's waiting room was of that genre—dark, a single chair. I had the sense that there was another room in the apartment where a patient who had preceded me was putting on a coat, or whatever, having just completed the bean-spilling process.

The psychiatrist sat behind a large desk. No couch or anything like that. I sat immediately in front of him, as if I were there to ask for a job. He was a large man, and when he leaned back in his chair, arranging his hands in a steeple, the chair squeaked alarmingly.

"A dab of oil will do it," I said—the first words to pass between us. His eyes widened slightly. I had put him on the defensive, I realized later, because I don't think he knew I was referring to the squeak in his chair. He never quite established the proper authoritarian relationship from that day on. Nor did my next sentence, which was: "What can I do for you?"

After the first month, I realized something—that my sole purpose in being there was to entertain him. I love telling stories. He was a willing listener. Sometimes he was visibly amused, his chair squeaking as he rocked back and forth. I told him about my adventures writing for *Sports Illustrated*. He was interested to hear about my literary friends. I told him about fishing off Boca Raton. I spent a session telling him about fireworks, a passion of mine. Each month he would slide a bill for his services across his big desk toward me with the tip of his fingers, watching my eyes as I picked it up.

Then one afternoon I began telling him about Mr. Wooster, his saxophone, and the night he slept under my friend's bed. I told him about the sea lions and how cold it was swimming in the quarry. As I left his office, with his folded bill in my pocket, I realized I had come full circle.

I think that is what is supposed to happen in the "shrink" business (there! I got it out!)—"closing the circle."

So I never went back.

DIANE ACKERMAN

ON TRANSFERENCE LOVE

This morning I went to the local deli for breakfast, and to spend time with Carol, a pretty, chestnut-haired, single woman in her forties. A zoologist, she had been away on an expedition, and we hadn't seen each other for many months. So we set out on a girlfriend expedition of our own, catching up on all the travels in each other's lives. In time, the conversation turned to her latest thought: going into therapy to construe some of the patterns in her life, and to find detours around the rocky relationships with men she always seems to plow into. She asked my advice about whether she should choose a male or female therapist, and, since she is the daughter of an alcoholic father who made her early life a misery, I suggested a male. She was fearful about having an intimate relationship with someone under such artificial circumstances. That got me thinking about the goals of psychotherapy.

Uppermost in a therapist's mind are such matters as not making the client worse; putting out any roaring fires; investigating difficult conflicts; helping the client become more stable, self-reliant, and self-accepting. But one aspect of a therapist's job is to develop a safe, stable, accepting relationship with a client, showing her by example what a healthy attachment would be like, in the hope that she will then be able to recognize its features and look for the same sort of relationship outside therapy.

"You believe their duty is to offer love to each client?" Carol asked.

"If they are any good, they are serial lovers."

"I'll be meeting this guy, intimately, twice a week," she said. "What if I fall in love with him? That's the standard joke, that you have to fall in love with your analyst, right?"

"Actually the standard joke is: How many psychologists does it take to change a lightbulb?"

"I give up," she said, slicing into a Mexican omelet.

"Only one. But the lightbulb has to *want* to change." We laughed as a waitress appeared with cups of hazelnut coffee.

"Falling for your therapist isn't required," I continued, "and many people don't feel anything of the kind. But the circumstance—meeting secretly in a quiet room with a man who is completely open to you at your most vulnerable, and with whom you share your fantasies, hurts, and dreams—that's very seductive, and it encourages love, it allows love to flourish."

"Suppose I fall head over heels in love with him, body and soul, hot and heavy?"

"That would be both agonizing and very helpful. True, you would find yourself in a diabolically painful, unrequited relationship with a man you feel physically rejected by, and yet have to meet regularly. You'd be sitting across from him, face-to-face, knowing that he knows how desperately you love him, and also knowing that he doesn't want you—it can't get much more humiliating than that. But you'd also have the unique luxury of being able to analyze your pain with him, pick out which elements hurt and why, which are based on reality, which are exaggerations and distortions, which reflect scars you are carrying from childhood or past relationships with other men."

"But there I would be, dying to have a real relationship with him, to do things together, to make love . . ."

"Let's suppose you get your wish. He gets sexually involved with you, and for a while that seems fabulous. He's most likely married, and the odds are that he's not going to leave his wife. I say this because statistically that's the picture—roughly 7 percent of male therapists have affairs with their clients, but only .01 percent of that figure go on to marry them. Soon enough all sorts of man/woman problems would arise. There you would be, having another bad relationship with a man. His job is not to add to your list of unsatisfactory relationships; it's to help you learn from them and avoid them. To that extent, he would have betrayed your trust. And, of course, it would make continuing therapy impossible. How would you feel if you were paying a man you were having sex with? Wouldn't that make you feel exploited? You would almost certainly end up in therapy with someone else just to deal with your bad relationship with your first therapist."

"All right, let's suppose I don't fall in love with him. A long time ago, I was in therapy briefly with a woman, and I couldn't bear the broken relationship at the end. Here you have this intense intimacy with someone you care for and trust, and then suddenly the reverse is true and you never see them again. I felt so disposed of; it was crushing."

"From the therapist's point of view, I guess that's the safest course to follow. Sometimes in novels or movies, strangers meet on a train and don't even tell each other their full names. But they have the freedom to be unparalleled lovers, acting out any fantasy, feeling unjudged and totally uninhibited. They can reveal anything, be anything. Psychotherapy is like that. Most therapists feel that they cannot become friends with their clients—even after therapy ends—because it would prevent that intense, liberating anonymity if the client should ever need to return for help. So their policy is: once an intimate always a stranger. Freud himself didn't practice this principle; over the years, he became dear friends with a few of his patients whom he particularly liked. They often socialized, and neither he nor they reported any problems resulting from the fullness of their friendship. Indeed, I know a psychiatrist in Manhattan, a wonderful woman in her seventies, who has outside friendships with some of her patients; and they

rave about her as a person and as an effective therapist. But that requires remarkable people who can compartmentalize exceptionally
well, and most therapists can't manage that, or don't want to as a general principle. In any case, you are having the most intimate relationship of your life with him, but he is having intimate relationships
with many people. His day is filled with tumultuous human dramas
and towering moments of empathy. Dealing with them often requires
pinpoint concentration. After hours, he undoubtedly wants to clear his
mind of all that, and for his own mental health he needs to. Probably
the last thing he wants is to fill his leisure time with the same psychic
carnage, or even with people who remind him of it. I very much doubt
that many therapists have relationships with their friends—or for that
matter with their families—which are as intense as the ones they have
with their clients."

"And yet you still believe it's worth doing, despite everything,
despite the ordeal."

"Because of the ordeal. Because learning how to love in a way
that's not self-destructive is essential for survival. At this point, your
world seems littered with hidden snares and bombs, some of which
life dropped when you weren't looking, and some of which you have
set for yourself. Defusing them is an ordeal. How could it be otherwise? But the world will be a safer place for you if you *can* defuse
them."

I knew I was sending her to her salvation, but perhaps also to considerable torment. In the ancient hieroglyphic poems, love is a secret. It
is so obsessive, so all-consuming, so much like insanity, that one is
ashamed to admit how much life one has surrendered. Caught in the
undertow of a powerful transference, Carol might not be able to reveal
to her therapist how much of her mental and emotional life he con-
sumes. Because she has a sensitive and tender heart, she will love him
honestly, beautifully, with all the ampleness of her spirit, but because
he will not return that love, or even comfortably acknowledge its seriousness and proportions, it will seem shameful. She may feel self-

hatred, since it seems to be her fault alone for loving him so one-sidedly. She will not understand that the love has formed—to use Stendhal's image—as naturally as a crystal of salt does on a branch in a sealed salt mine. She could not have stopped it; it did not arise because of some defect in her. It is an entity that sometimes grows in the caverns of psychotherapy, particularly if the therapist encourages it to flourish. But it will burn in her open wounds, it will torture her.

Carol may walk willingly into the primeval forest of deep transference, but will she be able to get out safely? Although neither is simple or without peril, it's marginally easier to leap onto a dragon's back than to climb off it. Dragons come naturally to mind because transference love is, in many ways, medieval in structure. It's a love heightened by obstacles, taboos, and impossibilities, as was courtly love. That makes it all the more delectable. The therapist is like a knight who must prove his devotion by *not* lying down with his lady. Or rather, in effect, by lying down with her but not touching her. That was, after all, the final and truest test of a knight's love, if he could steal into his lady's chamber and climb into bed beside her, while her naked body appealed to all his normal male appetites, without laying a hand on her. In therapy, the patient lies down—literally or figuratively—and is more naked than naked, more exposed than mere nudity could ever reveal. The therapist proves his devotion by not responding sexually. His quest is to restore what has been lost or stolen from the castle of her self-regard. It is a difficult task, which they both construe as a journey fraught with obstacles and danger and strife. There are dragons to slay. There are whirlwinds to tame. There are enemies without. There are monsters within.

EMILY FOX GORDON

MY LAST THERAPIST

When I remember Dr. B.'s office I envision it from an aerial angle. I see myself slightly hunched at one end of the comfortable leather couch. I see him flung back in his specially designed orthopedic rocker, his corduroy-sheathed legs outstretched, his ankles crossed, his bald pate gleaming. I see the two of us looking out from our lamp-lit island into a parcel of shadowy office space, in the direction of the darkened alcove where Dr. B. typed up his bills and displayed the photographs of his wife and children that, squint and peer and crane my neck as I might, I could never quite make out.

Dr. B. was a fit and pleasant-looking man in his early forties, with a rather long and slightly horsey face, a little like Prince Charles's, or a Semitic version of John Updike's. He emanated sensitivity and good-will and he had a fine speaking voice, an anchorman's baritone, which tended to lighten as he grew animated. When I first met him—nearly fifteen years ago—I was impressed by his handshake: a firm grasp, two hard pumps, and a quick release. By the time our acquaintance was five minutes old, I had formed an opinion of him that I never entirely abandoned, though I did revise and expand it: ordinary!

Dr. B. led me to his office, a small utilitarian space on the top floor of the local hospital. On the wall facing the patient's chair, he displayed his diplomas and a poster-sized photograph of a sailboat in a storm, its deck half-swamped and drastically tilted. He observed me as I took inventory of his office and smiled. "Checking things out?" he asked. "Yes, indeed," I answered. "As well you should!" he said, emphatically. I recognized the language of consumerism, then a fairly new trend in therapy.

Dr. B. declared himself available to work with me before the first session was over. His eagerness did not surprise me: I was a literary kind of person, wasn't I, and didn't he have a reputation as a psychiatrist with a special interest in literature and the arts? Surely I was brighter, I found myself thinking, than a lot of his patients, and more interesting. Reasonably stable, free of drug dependency, capable of humorous self-deprecation, even charm. And, almost simultaneously, I recoiled: was this what I had come to—finding gratification in the imagined prospect of becoming some shrink's prize patient? Surely I was too much of a veteran for that.

I

By the time I arrived in Dr. B.'s office I had been through five therapists, three before the age of seventeen. Two of these were almost comically inappropriate; between the ages of eleven and thirteen, I was the patient of two separate classically trained psychoanalysts.

The first was Dr. V., who was Viennese and practiced on the Upper East Side of Manhattan. Dr. V. kept a tank of exotic fish in her waiting room. She had mismatched eyes, one small and weepy, the other hypertrophied and glaucous, like an eye behind a jeweler's loupe. Dr. V. was followed by Dr. H., another middle-aged woman, but midwestern and more motherly. Like Dr. V., she put me on the couch and maintained a silence throughout the hour.

But she knitted me a sweater. The cables fell out of her needles fully articulated, like great ropes heaved length by length over the side of a ship. I appreciated the symbolism; the developing sweater was meant to suggest that something was being made here, that in spite of my nearly complete silence, progress of some kind was happening. At the end of my therapy with Dr. H.—why it stopped, I had no idea: I could only guess it was because the sweater was finished—she presented it to me. It was very handsome and unbecoming and smelled ever after of Dr. H.'s Pall Malls.

I failed in these early therapies, or attempts at analysis, as I suppose they should properly be called. How could I have succeeded? And what could Drs. V. and H. have been expecting? Thrown into deep waters without instruction, I floated mute, Dr. V.'s great eye like an implacable sun above me. My silence was both anxious and voluptuous. I felt a gentle pressure to speak, but I also felt pillowed by the assurance that silence was all right—good, in fact. It established my bona fides as a sensitive person, because only a sensitive person would remain silent when given the opportunity to speak. The more silence, the more certainty that the surface tension of the silence would break; the more prolonged the silence, the more import it would be seen, once broken, to have had. The first would be last and the last would be first: I had internalized this, the fundamental psychoanalytic dialectic, before I turned thirteen. On the couch I felt like a passenger on a night train, lying in a closed compartment on a gently rocking bed, passive and inert, but hurtled forward by the process of travel.

The waiting rooms of Drs. V. and H. had the feeling, for me, of sanctified space. I understood Dr. V.'s aquarium as a metaphor for the unconscious mind: those glittering bits of protein flashing through it—how I wished I could pinch the tails of their analogs in my brain, draw them out wriggling and present them to her.

I brought a free-floating ardor to my first encounters with psychotherapy, a kind of religious hunger that had gone unfed by my parents' agnosticism, their skepticism, their pragmatic liberalism. As I lay on the couch, my thoughts were runnels of dreamy speculation just below the translucent skin of consciousness, monitored, but not entirely registered. I never actually expressed these thoughts, not because I was secretive—nobody could have been more eager to reveal herself than I—but because I had childishly misunderstood the rules of free association. Somehow I had picked up the idea that only unconscious thoughts were to be spoken. An obvious contradiction, but I blurred this impossiblity into a kind of Zen *koan*. Once I had solved it, I felt sure that enlightenment would follow.

My therapeutic education broke off while I went away to boarding school for two years. After I was thrown out, I returned to Washington, D.C., where my parents then lived, and began therapy with Dr. G., my first male doctor. He was the most genuinely detached of all my therapists. When I remember him, I bring to mind a cartoonist's doodle-drawing of a shrink—one quick unbroken line describing a domed, balding head, continuing with a substantial hooked nose and receding chin, and petering out after tracing the swell of a modest professional's paunch. He had a wry decency that was mostly, but not entirely, lost on me at the time. He seemed, emotionally, to be a smooth dry surface; no burrs to snag my creepers or wet spots to which I might adhere.

My therapy with Dr. G. was the first in which I sat up and faced the therapist, the first in which I talked freely, and also the first in which I withheld or distorted the truth. I never mentioned how mortified I was, for example, to notice that the patient who walked out of his waiting room as I entered was a fat, obnoxious girl with alopecia and a steady rapid blink who went to my school, and I never confided my fear that perhaps Dr. G. had made the treatment of fat adolescent girls—I *was* fat, though not nearly as fat as she was—his specialty.

With Dr. G. I learned to "talk therapy." This was not a matter of using jargon—I'm proud to say I've never done that—but of recognizing which gambits and attitudes cause the therapist to signal his receptiveness. Even the most poker-faced practitioner will always reward an attentive patient with some small sign, a subtle alteration in the set of facial muscles, a dilation of the pupils. So, with Dr. G. I reached the "clever Hans" stage of my development as a patient.

And like the novice painter who has learned to use the entire canvas, I finally learned how to fill the hour; now I saw that anything I said could be depended on to color the silences that followed, giving them a plausible opacity behind which I could hide until I found another thing to say. Often I talked about loneliness, or feeling as if I were enclosed in a glass box. These themes seemed to engage Dr. G., and they gave me a pleasant feeling, too. I enjoyed the waiflike image I conjured up of myself, and the resultant gentle tide of self-pity that washed over me, raising the hair on my arms and leaving my eyes prickling with tears.

Throughout my three years as Dr. G.'s patient, I felt a guilty and unshakable conviction that I was completely sane and that I had health to squander. Of course, my notion that patients were expected to be crazy was a naive one, but I had swallowed whole the familiar ideology that connects madness to beauty of spirit. My knowledge of my strength and sanity was a secret I did my best to keep from Dr. G. I wanted him to see me as vulnerable and sensitive rather than robust. I loved the notion of myself as saucer-eyed and frail, and I was ashamed of the blunt and caustic person I knew I was. I hoped that if I applied myself, I might evolve toward becoming the fragile and purely lovable being I so wished to be. I was looking for transformation, not cure. I wasn't interested in being happier, but in growing more poignantly, becomingly, meaningfully unhappy.

Perhaps the reader wonders: why did my parents send me to these psychoanalysts at such an early age? My mother would have explained that my chronic underachievement in school was the reason, and later she would have added my bad and wild behavior (mild by today's standards).

And what was wrong with me? A family systems therapist would have identified me as the family scapegoat, the child designated to "act out" the conflicts between my tense, driven father and my incipiently alcoholic mother, the vent through which the collective rage escaped; a Winnicottian would point to the consequences of early maternal inadequacy (my mother was bedridden with phlebitis for most of my first year); a practitioner with a neurological bent could find evidence of a learning disability.

All these hypotheses have explanatory power. I tend to favor the last one, at least on days when I feel inclined to believe that there *is* such a thing as a learning disability. But they were all equally irrelevant to the reality of the adolescent I was. About her I can only say that if she was angry, she was also extremely passive, and mired in a deep helplessness, and that therapy became a means by which she became even more so.

My therapeutic education did me harm. It swallowed up years when I might have been learning, gathering competence, and undergoing the toughening by degrees that engagement in the world makes possible. Even worse was the effect of my therapies on my moral development: seedlings of virtues withered. An impulse that might have flowered, for example, into tact—the desire to gently investigate another's feelings—fell onto the stony ground of the therapist's neutrality and became manipulativeness, a tough perennial better suited to these desert conditions.

I acquired the habit of the analysand, the ruthless stripping away of defenses. But in my case not much self had yet developed, and surely none of it was expendable. I was tearing away not a hardened carapace, but the developing layers of my own epidermis. By reducing myself to a larval, infantile state I was doing what I felt I was expected to do, and what would please the therapist.

II

By the time I was sixteen I had given up any serious college ambitions. I spent the days sulking and smoking in the snack bar of a bowling alley with a group of fellow truants. At the age of eighteen, at loose ends and living with a boyfriend's mother in suburban Indianapolis, I scratched my wrists with a pair of nail scissors. The boyfriend's mother put me on a train the next day, and when I arrived in Washington my parents lost no time in taking me back to Dr. G., who suggested that I spend some time in a therapeutic community—an open psychiatric hospital in the Berkshires was his recommendation.

For years life had been retreating and the space it left, filling up with therapy; at Riggs life *was* therapy. Here I was surrounded by young people, most of them no more apparently disturbed than I was. Our physical circumstances were comfortable; we lived in private rooms in a big, high-ceilinged residence, ate good food, and were offered the usual diversions—volleyball and tennis, ceramics and woodworking. We were free to come and go.

From the first I felt something anomalous in our interactions with one another. It was as if we had been positioned at oblique angles to one another and had gotten stuck that way, unable to twist ourselves free so as to stand face-to-face. We had been planted in therapy, like rows of sunflowers. Our gazes were tilted upward, each toward the face of the therapist. Like acolytes at the feet of masters, we were taught to cultivate a contempt for the distractions that surrounded us. So we lived in communal loneliness and restless boredom. I can still "taste" these feelings; the sight of a jewel-green expanse of lawn or a hanging pot of pink and purple fuchsia can set them off in me as surely as an electrode probing brain tissue can evoke a hallucination

I stayed for three years, years I would otherwise have spent in college. I was assigned to an incompetent, neophyte research psychologist I'll call Dr. S. (number four in the running count). After the first year I became an outpatient and Dr. S., who was married and soon to become a father, began to show up at my door with bottles of wine and sheepish smiles. I got no help from the Riggs bureaucracy in my effort to extricate myself from this embroilment; firmly gripping my upper arm, the senior psychiatrists steered me out of their offices. One and all, they told me the same story: what I had mistaken to be Dr. S.'s feelings for me were merely projections of my own transference. Here I felt for the first time the chill of an encounter with psychiatry in its systematic aspect.

Then Leslie Farber arrived at Riggs, coming in to serve as director of therapy for the new administration. He listened to my complaint about Dr. S., believed me, and—eventually—took me on as a patient.

Dr. Farber never found Riggs congenial, and he left for New York after a little more than a year, taking me and two other patients with him. It is no exaggeration to say that Dr. Farber rescued us.

How difficult it is to abandon the ironic mode and speak enthusiastically! Although I list Dr. Farber as one in the succession of my shrinks, I do so apologetically, recognizing that this is a gross miscategorization—something like including Kafka in a roundup of Czech insurance underwriters. He was something other and larger than the rest of them, so much so that he eludes easy characterization. I write about him troubled by the well-founded fear that I will fail to do him justice.

He was a thinker and writer as well as a psychoanalyst, the author of two books of remarkable essays. His critique of psychoanalysis began with his understanding of human will, a category he believed had been "smuggled into" psychoanalytic explanations of motive without acknowledgment, an element anatomized in literature, philosophy, and theology, but neglected in psychoanalytic theory.

To understand people only in the reductive terms of the "medical model" was a drastic impoverishment of human possibility. Dr. Farber shared this belief with others associated with the humanistic or existential schools, but he never shared their woolly and inspirational leanings. He was tough-minded, pessimistic by temperament, and a man of deep emotional conservatism. He was a believer in God who protected his belief from all but the most serious inquirer.

Dr. Farber was in his late fifties when I met him. Though less ravaged, his small-chinned, delicate-boned eastern European face was nearly as seamed and pouched, expressive and revelatory of character, as W. H. Auden's at the same age. He was a small man, plump and sedentary, but his walk had verve and his motions were graceful. I remember the elegant and efficient way he handled his keys as he opened his office door, one eye squeezed shut against the updraft of smoke from the cigarette in the corner of his mouth.

He exuded melancholy and humor. His *gravitas,* his distinction, were so immediately and overwhelmingly apparent that even in my deteriorated and boredom-numbed condition I recognized them. It was a revelation to me, this full, rich, pungent, complex humanity. It was as if another self continued to live inside the therapeutic self I had become, lying slack but fully jointed, waiting for some salutary yank to spring alive.

My sessions with Dr. Farber were entirely unlike my earlier experience of therapy. I had learned to think of my utterances as soap bubbles rotating in midair, to be examined by me with the help of the therapist. They were the matter of the enterprise. But with Dr. Farber, no such "work" was being undertaken. Instead, we talked. He talked—for example—about his childhood in Douglas, Arizona, and how growing up in the desert had affected his inner life. We talked about his marriages, my boyfriends, his children, my parents, his dismay at watching Riggs patients, most of them young and few really sick, loitering in a psychiatric limbo. We talked about movies and TV and the youth culture; we gossiped freely about the Riggs staff and patients. Dr. Farber expected me to hold up my end of these conversations, to keep him interested. Was I up to it? Mostly, but not always.

My reaction to my earliest view of Dr. Farber's world was something like the "wild surmise" of stout Cortez's men at their first sight of the Pacific. I knew quite suddenly not only that this world was *there* but also what that signified. This was my first apprehension of the realm of the moral, about which my parents had taught me very little and therapy had taught me nothing.

The notion that another person might have a moral claim on me, or that I might have such a claim on another, was a novel one. So was the idea that a moral worldview had an intellectual dimension that required the careful working out of distinctions, the most significant of which was the distinction between the moral and the aesthetic. This is the one I had, and still have, the greatest trouble understanding. Is there such a thing as a moral style? It has always troubled and confused me that Dr. Farber's influence on me had so much to do with traits that were really more aesthetic than moral—his worldly panache, his toughness.

With Dr. Farber I felt free to express the caustic and humorous judgments I had been squelching for years. He enjoyed and encouraged my rude health. The world, which my therapeutic existence at Riggs had bleached of color and emptied of content, began to fill up again.

III

My move from Austen Riggs to New York City was a jarring transition. I wanted life, unfiltered and unprocessed? Here it was, the real thing, lonely, grubby, and full of jolts. I lost jobs, lived in chaos, and kept my money in a bureau drawer. My gums bled and my menstrual cycle went haywire. I cut my hair myself to save money, and the result made me look like the mental patient I had been pretending to be at Riggs. I got robbed, mugged, raped. At one point, the cockroach colony in my apartment grew so large that it produced an albino strain—translucent creatures whose internal workings were visible in certain lights.

I was living on my own and I simply did not do very well. I had envisioned an exhilarating life in some vaguely imagined bohemia. But there was no bohemia anymore, none that I could find. Instead, there was poverty and disorder and a series of bizarre low-paying jobs that seem funny and picaresque only in retrospect.

Dr. Farber charged me an income-adjusted fee of $7.50 a session. He and his wife went out of their way to help me get established in New York; they paid me handsomely to stay with their children while they went to Paris for a week, and during one of my homeless intervals Dr. Farber arranged for me to sleep on a cot in his brother's empty studio. They fed me regularly. How warm and inviting the prospect of roast chicken at their table seemed as I sat on the clanking, hissing subway train, fighting the temptation to get off at the Farbers' Upper West Side stop, how appealing when contrasted to my hot plate, my canned chili and saltines, my cockroaches. And, indeed, it was wonderful to spend time in that bustling, musical, intellectually lively household, which eventually came to serve as a sort of salon for a certain group of New York intellectuals.

Other patients also visited the apartment and got to know the family—Dr. Farber never observed the psychiatric taboo against associating with patients, and for him therapy and friendship were inextricable. But I grew dependent on the Farber household, and as my dependency deepened I grew closer to Dr. Farber's wife and more distant from him. I often felt that he was getting sick of me, always there as I was, in his office and in his home, across the room and across the table, even asleep on the family couch, inhibiting his habit of wandering through the apartment late at night in darkness.

I knew that my contributions to our talks had grown stilted and falsely animated—"willed," as Dr. Farber would have put it. I found that I suddenly had very little to say. The struggles of my daily life—getting to work on time under threat of being fired, making it to the Laundromat, avoiding crime, and trying to stay clean when the hot water in my building was more often off than on—all this had apparently drained my head of anything interesting. I arrived at Dr. Farber's comfortable Riverside Drive office, with its high views of the streaky Hudson, blinking in the strong light, feeling dirty and uncertain about how I smelled.

The fact is, I had very little to offer. My education had been so impoverished, so radically incomplete, that I had grown up to be a creature of hunches and blurts, and soon even these had dried up. My sketchy views had long since been outlined and exhausted, and all I had to give back to Dr. Farber were flimsily disguised recapitulations of his own.

George Eliot, in a reference to phrenology, the psychology of her day, once spoke of her oversized "Organ of Veneration." Apparently I had one, too. I became a furtive taxonomist, dividing up the world into the Farberian and the non-Farberian. What was Farberian I would embrace; what was non-Farberian I would reject. But sometimes—frequently—I got it wrong. Once I told Dr. Farber that I wanted to explore Orthodox Judaism. What I knew of his own tightly guarded belief and his interest in Martin Buber gave me confidence that this would please him. Dr. Farber looked at me with amused incredulity: "You want to wear a wig?" he said. "You want to take a ritual bath every month? Seriously?"

Daniel was another of Dr. Farber's patients in New York, an intellectually promising and sensitive young man with a yeshiva background who, like me, had languished for several years at the upstate hospital, his prognosis growing steadily worse, before Dr. Farber came along to rescue us.

I had found a job, my most respectable yet, as a glorified coffee fetcher and Xeroxer in the Academic Placement office at Columbia, where Daniel had resumed his interrupted education. I often ran into him on Broadway, at Chock Full o'Nuts and in the bookstores. We talked sometimes on the phone, and though we were not intimate, we maintained a concern for each other's fortunes in the city, a kind of sibling connection.

For a year or so, Daniel stayed on the dean's list, but then something gave way in his life and he began to skip classes. Eventually, he dropped out. During one of our phone conversations, Daniel sheepishly confided to me that he had not yet told Dr. Farber about this. A year passed, and Daniel continued the deception. I mentioned this to Dr. Farber's wife, during one of our cozy late-night gossips after the children had been put to bed. She passed the information to Dr. Farber, who confronted Daniel during his next session. They agreed that their friendship had been ended by the lie, and parted ways.

The explosion, when it came, was directed at me. I noticed, as Dr. Farber ushered me quickly into his office—no leisurely small talk, no smiles—that he looked grim and haggard, as if he had not slept well. I began to feel anxious, and I searched my mind frantically. Had I forgotten to pay? Had my check bounced?

I knew that Daniel had been dismissed. In fact, I had come to Dr. Farber's office that morning glowing with schadenfreude and braced

by the prospect of a ready-made interesting discussion. I was even prepared to plead Daniel's case a little; I wanted to remind Dr. Farber
about Daniel's history, the oppressively high expectations of his parents, the overshadowing intellectual success of his older brother.

So it was disturbing to me that Dr. Farber stared at the floor. His
reaction to my introductory stammerings was a long silence. When he
finally raised his head and engaged my eyes, his face was full of angry
puzzlement. "How could you . . .," he began, then shook his head and
fell silent. I was already weeping.

When he spoke again his voice was low and hoarse, his speech
ragged, as if he were vocalizing only random chopped-off segments of
a tormented thought process. But I got the idea. I had colluded with a
lie, which had compromised my friendship with Dr. Farber, and my
whisperings to his wife had in turn contaminated, if only briefly, even
his marriage: "How could you come into my home and . . . solicit . . .
my wife?"

I had meanwhile pitched myself out of my chair onto my knees.
Panic and grief had transported me, busted up some internal logjam,
and for the first time in months I spoke fluently to Dr. Farber as I
crouched on the carpet, sobbing, tears springing from my eyes.

"Please forgive me," I said. I had forgotten. Or maybe I never
learned. "Never learned what?" asked Dr. Farber. "That things matter," I said. For the first time since I had entered his office, Dr. Farber
looked at me as if I were a fellow-creature. "Yes, they do," he said, and
I was so relieved at this turning that I burst into fresh sobs.

Instantly, I understood that I had gotten it wrong, unconsciously
slipped back to the precepts of my early therapeutic education. I had
reverted to understanding the relationship between Dr. Farber and
Daniel, between Dr. Farber and me, as a game played for therapeutic
chips, not as a reality in which human connection was at stake.

Of course, Dr. Farber had gotten it wrong, too—I think now—
because my silence on the subject of Daniel's deception had as much to
do with simple reluctance to be a snitch as any larger failure to honor
human relatedness. It was quite innocent, really, and perhaps I should

have defended myself against Dr. Farber's unexpected and misdirected anger, which shocked me so much that I was unable to properly assimilate its meaning. It was guilt at my own bad faith—my desperate clutching at a friendship which I knew had ended—that found expression in my tearful contrition.

Dr. Farber granted me a kind of amnesty, but never, I think, real forgiveness. He waved me out of his office with an air of preoccupied disgust, but I could sense that in his exasperation his sense of humor had wanly reasserted itself. Before I left I won from him the assurance that I could return the next week.

I envied the seriousness of Daniel's transgression. I suspected that Dr. Farber cared more about Daniel than me; his anger was like a father's toward a beloved errant son. And, like an errant son, Daniel had been cut decisively free; he left New York and moved to Israel, joined the army, and married there, returning to the States years later with his young family. His dismissal from Dr. Farber's office left him bereft, but it also served to jolt him out of a rut. He got to keep, I think, some of his legacy from Dr. Farber, while my lesser, weaker, more equivocal offense kept me tied to Dr. Farber for another year, during which I used mine up.

Or so I understood myself to be doing. Meanwhile, I had found a boyfriend and moved in with him. This boyfriend, who was later to become my husband, took a satirical view of my attachment to Dr. Farber. He often compared me to a character in one of R. Crumb's underground comic books, the goofy, loose-limbed Flakey Foont, always in pursuit of his guru, Mr. Natural, an irascible little visionary in flowing robes with a white beard and giant, flapping bare feet. At the end of that year, my wedding a few months off, I ended things with Dr. Farber myself. I confessed to him that I had had little to say to him for years. I needed to leave, I told him, because I was in danger of becoming the acolyte who gets the master's message wrong. I knew how little Dr. Farber wished to serve as my guru, and I knew how particularly inappropriate my idealizing impulse toward him was. His tendency was deflationary: he nearly always preferred a modest exactitude to a rapturous generality.

I can see myself, I said, twenty years from now as a barfly, the regular who climbs onto her stool every afternoon at two and by four o'clock is mumbling to anyone who will listen the incoherent tale of the wise man she once knew in her youth. Dr. Farber accepted my resignation with warmth. My confession was true, and he liked it because it was true, and because it had a self-immolating boldness calculated to appeal to him. I offered it not because it was true, but because it was the only way I knew to please him.

IV

When, twelve years after I exiled myself from Dr. Farber, I first walked into Dr. B.'s office, I was just emerging from the sea of early motherhood onto some indeterminate shore. I felt that my relation to the future had undergone a subtle change, one which signaled, I can see in retrospect, the onset of middle age. I found I lacked, and had been lacking for longer than I wanted to admit, the unshakable confidence in my own sanity and stability that I had once considered such an embarrassing encumbrance. I felt a vague sense of balked urgency. My husband and I were constantly fighting. I brought with me a tangle of confusion and sadness about Dr. Farber, who had recently died.

Dr. B. passed one crucial test during the first session. He recognized Dr. Farber's name and knew a little about him. "Irreplaceable," he said, "lifesaving," and I loved him for that. He went on to link Dr. Farber with my father, who had also died recently. "A lot of loss," he said, shaking his head deploringly. My reaction was mild disappointment and annoyance. I didn't like the idea of packaging Dr. Farber and my father together, but I let it pass.

Then, a few weeks later, Dr. B. said something almost unforgivable; he interrupted one of my many anecdotes about Dr. Farber with what he called "a reality consideration." Dr. Farber, he said, had been well known in the profession as a sufferer from depression. Wasn't it possible, he suggested, that during my years as Dr. Farber's patient, I had tried to compensate him for his sadness, just as I had done with my unhappy mother?

How many things could be wrong with this? Could anything be right? First, the "reality consideration": was it implied here that the profession had a corner on reality? And depression: Dr. Farber had had his own views about depression. I suggested that Dr. B. go to the library and look them up. What the profession took to be Dr. Farber's depression was actually despair.

But I was too angry to argue; instead I picked up the first wad of *ad hominem* that came to hand and flung it in Dr. B.'s direction. I looked up at the ship photograph. That put me in mind of an analogy; I compared Dr. Farber to an ocean-going liner with a great, deep hull, and Dr. B. to a surface-skimming Sailfish. Two spots of bright pink appeared just below Dr. B.'s cheekbones, and I pointed them out to him, literally pointed with my finger, all the while registering in one corner of my mind the appalling rudeness of the gesture.

I was working myself into a rage, and I could see that he was calculating how best to backtrack and calm me down. He threw up his hands. "O.K.," he said. "You're quite right. I was out of line. I'm not perfect. Do you need me to be perfect?"

"No," I said. "I need you to be smart." Dr. B. absorbed that without comment and we sat in silence for several minutes. I was registering my disgust at the hokeyness of the "I'm not perfect" line and the seductive pseudointimacy of "Do you need me . . . ?" I was also fuming at the realization that Dr. B. had saved his remarks about Dr. Farber until he had me well roped in as a patient. He had waited until it seemed safe to introduce his revisionist agenda. He was getting off, no doubt, on the idea of rescuing me from my thralldom to a distinguished dead practitioner; this was the old supplanter's story so familiar to the profession.

Here I was, seated in the office of my sixth therapist. Hadn't I decided, with Farber's help and long ago, that what I needed was to recover *from* therapy? Why, then, was I even here? One thing I was *not* doing was undertaking a revision of my views of Dr. Farber. This was such a touchy subject that Dr. B. never raised it again. The dismay I felt at my own ugly and fluent anger was apparently to be punishment for my recidivist slide back into psychotherapy, for my bad faith.

In the early months with Dr. B., I assumed a new persona. I became hostile and prickly. I sneered at the nautical decor in his new office, especially the coffee table, which was a sheet of glass affixed to an old lobster trap. I took out after his ties, particularly a forest-green one with a pattern of tiny mud boots and the legend "L. L. Bean." It's not lost on me, by the way, that the sadistic and grandiose tendency of my behavior toward Dr. B. was the mirror image of the masochistic self-abnegation I had shown with Dr. Farber.

I behaved unpleasantly because I was paying to behave any way I pleased, and also because this was my emotionally primitive way of staying loyal to Dr. Farber. I would never have felt free to be so nasty if I had not been supremely confident of Dr. B.'s regard for me. It was, after all, overdetermined; Dr. B. told me that his positive feelings for me were highly useful to our work together, as were my negative ones for him. He explained that he could not will affection for a patient, but if he happened to feel it he made sure to cultivate it for the sake of the therapy.

Dr. B. kept his face in profile, his eyes lowered and shadowed, but he inclined his large listening ear toward me, and somehow he used that appendage expressively; something about its convoluted nakedness reassured and invited me. He also had a particular gift—how he learned to do this I can't imagine—for conveying, simply by sitting there, a warm satisfaction in the fact of my existence. His body's attitude seemed to say, "You're quite something, all right!"

Dr. B.'s physical expressiveness sometimes betrayed him; his face colored easily, and I could often see a look of eager anxiety spring into his eyes just as he was about to offer an interpretation. I liked him better silent than talking, because when he spoke he sometimes said the wrong thing, jarring me out of my meditations. His unquestioning acceptance of the tenets of his profession often angered me, and so did the way he turned my challenges back on me by engaging their emotive content rather than their substance.

The only topic I was willing to talk about in more or less conventional therapeutic terms was my marriage. Here Dr. B. acted like an advocate, pushing me to articulate my rancors and to assert what he saw as fundamental rights. He threw into question all my efforts to accommodate my husband's needs—What about *yours?* was his refrain. Of course, I enjoyed being the innocent one, the hotly defended one, but I knew that if my husband were the patient he would receive the same treatment—at least if Dr. B. had determined this to be in his therapeutic interest. I was dismayed by Dr. B.'s lack of concern for the complex, nuanced picture of my marriage—indeed, of the whole "life-world" that I was struggling to present. Often I felt as if I had spent the better part of the hour constructing an elaborate imaginary house, trying always to balance a wing of self-justification with one of judicious self-criticism, only to watch Dr. B. carelessly kick the thing over in his hunt for the hurt.

Dr. B.'s advocacy was gratifying, but it unnerved me deeply. To feel rancor was to feel self-pity, and I feared being caught up in its familiar dialectic. The more I struggled against it, the more touchingly valiant I appeared to myself, and the further I felt myself sucked back into a destructive self-cherishing. I learned to hate a certain look on Dr. B.'s face, a steady wide-eyed gaze qualified by a faint, enigmatic smile. I'm waiting patiently, his face said, for you to come off it. To him, my resistance to self-pity was simply a form of denial. To me, resistance was necessary; if I yielded to the seductions of self-pity, my efforts to construct a self would collapse and I would find myself falling back into a kind of watery Boschian hell, a bog where I would rot slowly in a solution of my own tears.

Dr. B. and I were talking past each other. When I asked whether my marriage was a good one or not, he understood me to be asking, "Is it good for me?" I wanted to know the answer to that question, but I was really after something else, something that I can only phrase, awkwardly, as follows: is my marriage part of "the good"? It should hardly have surprised me that from him I got psychological answers to philosophical questions.

V

I think of Dr. B. as a *tinted* man, an updated and affectively colorized version of the psychoanalytic "gray man." In his office I never endured the silences of Drs. V., H., and G. He was quick to move into relation with me, to offer me a kind of friendship. He was frank about the uses of this relationship: it would serve as a kind of mock-up. Our work together would consist not only of shuffling through my past, but also of examining our own relationship for patterns and tendencies applicable to my outside life. What about his own patterns?, I asked. Wouldn't they complicate the matter? I could trust him, he assured me, not to let his own needs intrude, or if that was impossible, to inform me of their presence. This he did, sometimes rather oddly. When I was talking, for example, about having been raped when I lived in New York, he interrupted me and confessed that this story was making him very anxious, and that I should probably discount any reaction he offered.

Dr. B. operated under an extraordinary constraint, which was to keep his own humanity out of our relationship unless it served a therapeutic purpose. If that was not possible, if some errant tendril worked loose and struggled past the therapeutic boundary, it was subject to examination and extirpation on the spot. But he was also quite free to stir up my feelings deliberately, to flirt, to manipulate, to do any and all of these things as long as they were justified by the realistic expectation that they would serve a therapeutic end.

For my part, I was also severely limited. I was free, of course, to express anything, but the rules of the game did not allow me, like Dr. B., to manipulate without disclosure. I was also obliged to live with the knowledge that what transpired in Dr. B.'s office, however powerful its emotional charge, was not real. Dr. B. was fond of saying that what went on between us was *very* real, but of course the use of the intensifying "very" immediately threw up scare quotes around the "real."

Therapeutic gerrymandering had shaped the territory of our relationship strangely. Between us we had it all covered, but the shared portion was nearly nonexistent. Everything was possible between us—everything, that is, but mutuality. It's not exactly accurate to say that I longed for that crucial element—I was too wary of Dr. B. really to miss it much.

What I did feel was an intensification of my growing disgust at myself for having returned to therapy like the proverbial dog to his vomit, and for staying in therapy in spite of that disgust. After all, I knew better! I knew that whatever its ends, therapy was a sad, manipulative parody of authentic relation. But I also knew that in the outside world, therapeutic notions had become so omnipresent and pervasive as to be inescapable.

Why did I go back into therapy? I was very unhappy when I sought out Dr. B., but I don't believe that unhappiness was the cause of my return. I think it was more a pervasive social loneliness that herded me back, a sense of panicky disconnection from a central social tradition—a feeling to which young mothers have become particularly susceptible.

I believe I returned to therapy not only because it had been my element for so much of my life, but because it was the place I had seen everybody *else* go. By the time I became Dr. B.'s patient, therapy had overflowed its professional vessels, flooded the culture, and seeped into the groundwater. However I resisted it, every one of my interactions—as wife, daughter, sister, friend, and especially as mother—was subject to mediation by my own therapeutic notions and those of others. I was like an ex-smoker trapped in an unventilated designated smoking area, inhaling so many secondhand fumes that continued abstinence seemed pointless. I returned to therapy because, in a sense, I was already *in* therapy, but I felt myself to be placed uncomfortably on its periphery rather than securely inside it. I went back into therapy because it had become the central institution, the hearth, of my society.

Once, when I had been agonizing about my husband and the difficulty of keeping myself from being swamped by the intensity of his ambition, the vehemence of his anxiety, I ended my catalog of complaint by saying, "But he's a good person." Dr. B. leaned forward and whispered, in audible italics, *"You've never said anything different!"* At this I burst into tears of gratitude. I was touched that Dr. B. had been keeping track and that he handed me back the raw data in such a generous spirit.

In retrospect, it seems to me that this incident marked an end to the struggle between Dr. B. and me and the beginning of a real, if very minimal, friendship. Human nature is such, after all, that given time and proximity, mutuality will take root even in the least hospitable of environments.

More and more—as the leaves turned red and yellow outside Dr. B.'s windows, as fast-food restaurants and discount outlets sprang up on the outskirts of the small New England city where we all lived, as the snow flew and the years passed and my daughter grew and my husband wrote his books and my hair began to turn gray—I did the talking. I did the interpreting, too, in my own terms. My hand was on the tiller and I was yawing wildly all over the lake in my maneuverable little Sailfish, and it was fun. It occurs to me now that perhaps one of my many motives for returning to therapy was a desire to try my mettle against it, to seize control of therapy for my own purposes.

My talking was mostly narrative and descriptive; I went on at great length about faces, recounted events in intricate detail. When I spoke analytically or speculatively, I did so in general or philosophical, rather than psychological, terms. Sometimes Dr. B.'s eager-to-interpret look flashed momentarily across his face, but I could usually depend on him to quash the impulse. What I had begun to do, of course, in his office, was to write aloud.

In the years since I left Dr. B.'s office, I've begun to write in earnest, and writing has allowed me—as nothing else ever has or could—to escape the coils of therapy. I don't mean that writing has been therapeutic, though sometimes it has been. The kind of writing I do now is associative and self-exploratory—much like the process of therapy, except that the therapist is absent and I've given up all ambition to get well.

Let me give Dr. B. his due. He was more than competent; he was really good at what he did, and got better as he went along. Eventually, he became a kind of adept. He learned to vaporize at will like the Cheshire cat, leaving nothing behind but a glow of unconditional positive regard, allowing me a spacious arena in which to perform my dance of self. In resisting his impulse to lure me back into the charted territory of psychoanalytic explanation, he granted me my wish to be released into the wilds of narrative.

VI

Once, five or six years before I became Dr. B.'s patient, I left my husband and took the bus from our town in Vermont to New York City. I moved in with an ex-roommate, found another job at Columbia, and made an appointment with Dr. Farber.

He had given up his office now, and was seeing patients at the apartment. When I arrived, late in the afternoon, he shook my hand cordially and led me through the living room, past the familiar row of big, dusty windows overlooking West End Avenue and into the kitchen, where he fixed us both old-fashioneds. I stood at the counter and watched the assembly process, the slicing of the orange and lemon, which he carefully dotted with drops of bitters and sprinkled with sugar, the "muddling" with the back of a spoon, and the pouring of a jigger-and-a-half of good bourbon into each sturdy glass.

We retired to Dr. Farber's study with our drinks in hand. When I asked Dr. Farber for permission to smoke—he had suffered a stroke a few years earlier, and had given up his cigarettes—he encouraged me to do so, and to blow the smoke his way. When I told Dr. Farber of my decision to leave my marriage, he nodded gravely and with evident approval—he was no fan of marital strife.

I had a sudden impression that in the five years since I'd last seen him, Dr. Farber had moved into old age. He looked wryer, more elfin, a little in need of a haircut. The essential strength and depth of his spirit were still present, but it seemed to me that he had begun to conserve and protect himself. The *Sturm und Drang* of my life was only one of many clamorings, I felt sure, from which he had now begun, gently but implacably, to turn away.

When I asked Dr. Farber if he would take me on as a patient once again, he said no. We continued to talk for another half hour, reminiscing about Riggs and my New York days, and the tone of our talk was warm and relaxed. I returned to my husband and my life in Vermont a few days later. The news of his death reached me five years later, when I happened upon his obituary in *The New York Times*.

The last two years of my therapy with Dr. B. were marked by a long wrangle about what he called "the termination process." We had not yet entered this phase, he cautioned, and so the end of therapy could not yet be envisioned. How far away in time was the beginning of the termination phase from the end of therapy? That varied, said Dr. B. How would we know that the process had begun? When the work of therapy had been completed.

But it seemed that under the terms of our therapeutic détente, the work of therapy could never begin, and so, of course, it could never end. I could go on writing aloud, basking in the warmth of Dr. B.'s unconditional positive regard forever, or until my insurance ran out.

Real life intervened in the form of my husband's sabbatical leave. Dr. B. and I both accepted this as a stalemate-breaker, and the termination process was compressed into a few summer months just before my family's yearlong removal to Princeton. During these last sessions,

Dr. B. often interrupted my monologues to introduce the theme of attachment and loss, but the stream of my thought continued to ripple along as it always had, picking up no traces of this effluent.

So it was a surprise when at the end of our last session, just as I was about to stand up, Dr. B., who since our initial handshake seven years earlier had never once touched me, rose from his orthopedic rocker and stood before me. In what took me a moment to realize was a clumsy, mistimed attempt at a hug, he grasped my head in his hands and pressed it against his stomach, hard enough so that I could hear the gurgle of his digestion and feel his belt buckle bite into my cheek.

Never have I felt such a congestion of sensations; only in retrospect can I separate and order my reactions—first bewilderment, then a panicky vicarious embarrassment, then a flash of sexual arousal quickly extinguished by my realization that Dr. B.'s embrace was an awkward eruption of affection and not a pass, then a suffusion of amusement and tenderness. I got to my feet and returned Dr. B.'s hug, planted a kiss on his cheek, and left the office.

E. ETHELBERT MILLER

PLAYING CATCH WITH MYSELF

I'm throwing twice as hard as I ever did.
It's just not getting there as fast.
—Lefty Gomez

When my bad days begin to add up, I think of myself not as being depressed but rather as being in a slump. I think of myself as a baseball player not being able to hit the curveball or slider. I arrive at the ballpark each day, certain that I can get a hit. I struggle with my batting stance while taking note of how many points my average has dropped. Sometimes I sit at my desk or fall across the bed unable to write, and then the realization sets in that I've been here before and nothing is getting better. I need to be on the bench.

Several years ago, before I was a father, my wife suggested very strongly that I needed to be in therapy. No I said, but yes I did. Her reason for recommending it perhaps was linked to her desire to be in a healthy relationship. It was also an outgrowth of her own experiences with counseling. When we first met, my wife was seeing a therapist on a regular basis. She was one of the first African Americans I knew who was seeing a therapist even though she had not suffered from some type of emotional breakdown. Maybe the cost, or the fact that most therapists were white, kept many African Americans from seeking help. I knew many friends whose lives had fallen apart and they never reached out for help. A few had become homeless and our eyes eventually avoided each other's when we passed in the street.

My wife believed that therapy was necessary and essential to maintaining a balanced life. Reducing stress and examining the past in order to understand the present and make plans for the future were things she was committed to doing. Now and then she would share with me a few of the things she discussed with her therapist. She was gaining a better understanding of her childhood and hidden fears. I don't believe I expressed any real interest in knowing more. Like many people, my image of therapy consisted of lying on a couch and talking to someone who might not be listening but wanted to help if I could just be clear on what I needed. What did I need? How do you teach someone to hit a curve?

When I was a young boy growing up in the Bronx, my friend Dinky convinced his mother to let him join the Little League. I was a much better baseball player than Dinky, but my mother refused to let me sign up. I can still remember Dinky in his baseball uniform and how he went to several games without getting a chance to play. Then one afternoon he came home with fear painted on his face. He had a chance to hit in a game and saw his first real curveball. Dinky's description of a hardball sailing at his head and then slipping down over the plate was told with simple horror. Dinky's baseball career was over, and as I watched him holding his glove and punching his fist into the pocket, I wondered if I would have done any better.

It has always been my wife's belief that my father, Egberto Miller, an African American, suffered from depression. I grew up listening to my father holding conversations with himself while sitting in his bedroom or at the dinner table. "Mumbling to himself" was how my mother described it. I seldom saw my father talking on the phone or entertaining any friends. My father was a loner. He seemed to talk to no one, not even my mother. Even today, I look back on my childhood and can only recall a handful of conversations I had with him. My father was a man of many secrets. His mumblings were never recorded or transcribed. I have no recollection of what bothered him. Was it his work or the difficulty of providing for his family? Was it his relationship with my mother?

I cannot imagine my father rising early on a Saturday morning and deciding that instead of going outside to wash the car, he would take the train from the Bronx into Manhattan to visit a therapist. Everyone was a stranger to my father. He believed a person had no true friends, only acquaintances. Who would listen to my father? How many black men his age, with little formal education, hard workers and family providers struggling to survive, could have had the luxury of being in therapy? For a man who found it difficult to talk to his neighbors, it would have been impossible to talk to someone in an office who was there to help his mind and not his aching back.

I think of my father as one of those utility infielders every baseball team once had on their roster. A quiet guy who could play several positions, he would enter a game during the late innings for defensive purposes or because a starter was injured. These were players whose cards you were surprised to find in the small packages with the bubblegum. They were guys who were included in those big baseball trades along with relief pitchers and minor-leaguers. Their stories are often blues songs sung in stadiums during rain delays.

My father loved to listen to jazz. This was his music of relaxation. He met my mother at the old Savoy Ballroom in Harlem. I can see them on the dance floor together. My father's hand around my mother's waist. Their bodies touching for the first time. Both of them are shy, and my father searches for something to say after the music stops. He bends forward to whisper something into my mother's ear: a secret, perhaps, or maybe just the first words that will breathe life into my brother, my sister, myself.

How many wives become their husband's therapist? Listeners. Too often, attempts at conversations replacing lovemaking and sex. My father alone in the bedroom mumbling while my mother is in the kitchen opening cabinets and turning on the stove.

I grew up with both of my parents and I never thought about their relationship until maybe my own marriage. Suddenly, it seemed I was a husband, in a second marriage and a father of two children, and one day I caught myself mumbling about nothing in particular. I was talking to myself; maybe this is what I think about when I think of the possible importance of therapy.

Therapy is an opportunity, I suspect, to talk with oneself while talking to another person. A form of meditation, of listening, learning how to breathe, and letting go. It is the realization that emotional stability is a tightrope and that the ability to maintain one's balance is essential for celebrating the joy of living.

I never played catch with my father. He had no interest in sports. He ignored what I considered to be most important events: the pennant races and the World Series. How could you miss Mazeroski's homer and go to work the next day as if nothing had happened? My father did, and I still think of him as someone who got a big curve thrown at him by life.

It is only today, approaching fifty and having written a considerable number of poems and essays, that I think about what my life has meant. I look back on the deaths of my father and my brother, a failed first marriage, a second marriage, the birth of my son and daughter. I think of how similar my own life is to my father's. I see myself as being as much of a loner as he was. I am different from my father only in the amount of education I have received and the type of work I do.

Being a writer has made me very introspective. And in the process of writing, I have found myself sharing secrets rather than keeping them. Each poem has been a personal exploration into feelings and beliefs. I have found myself digging deeper over the years. I have returned to themes rooted in my childhood and buried under the playgrounds of New York. I have guided my muse as much as I have learned to listen to my heart. To write is to love. I could never imagine someone helping me do this. How could someone better guide me toward my own feelings? This is what my work has allowed me to do, especially during the last three years. My wife still maintains that I would benefit from therapy. We once agreed to see a counselor to help improve our relationship, but this ended with both of us talking less, not more. I guess it was like the Cuban missile crisis or the blockade, something that changes your history forever. It was the only effort I ever made to sit down with someone outside my family and discuss my problems.

Some of my friends might raise the issue of race and culture as a reason for my reluctance. Both my parents have family that link them to the Caribbean. They are island people, folks who are surrounded by water. Maybe this is a reason for detachment. On Sundays, when I was small, my entire family took the long trip to Brooklyn, where we were surrounded with accents, wonderful food, and cousins you could lock in bathrooms. Even now as I write this, I can still remember my mother reminding me to wash my hands before eating. I can see my father sitting in the corner wishing he was somewhere else. He was a very private and religious man. His faith would have a strong influence on my older brother, who entered a monastery in the early sixties. Yet I also have memories of my father's anger exploding through our small apartment on Longwood Avenue. There were enough of these outbursts to convince a small child like myself that I would be a fool to get in my father's way.

There is so much I don't know about my father. What could I tell a therapist today? I don't know. Much of my childhood is clouded by whispers. I lack the memory my sister has. She can recall names, places, incidents that happened to everyone in the family. She knows stories while I attempt to reclaim fragments of my past and my beginnings, poem by poem.

So, I have started to reinvent myself; to claim a past as mythical as my father's first arrival in this country from Panama. As writers, many of us tell interviewers, and perhaps even our therapists, things we could best save for books. I feel comfortable stepping off first base and taking a lead. I have learned how to watch the pitcher. I like to listen to the roar of the crowd as I start to run . . . my cap flying from my head as if I were Willie Mays. My mind as pure as a dream.

DR. J. CATCHES THE BUS

"Anybody who would go to see a psychiatrist ought to have his head examined," Samuel Goldwyn said—a Hollywood solipsism that Freud would have neatly nailed as resistance. In fact, an entire generation of Americans has done just that. It was on the couch that we boomers learned to boom, that the "Me" decade perfected its self-absorption, and that we grew into a generation of adults obsessed with childhood. We turned to psychiatry and its investigation of remembered experience for everything once provided by religion, family, and community.

The postwar optimism that washed across America, settling in fertile golden eddies in the suburbs, was activated by the primitive idea that life made sense. Problems were just preludes to solutions—the way the Depression had been a prelude to prosperity and the war had been a prelude to a safe world: a world of two-car garages and moms baking in the kitchen and martinis at six. Political problems would be solved by the government. Personal problems would be solved by our shrinks, navigators of the perilous journey from ego to id and back again. Traveling to the unconscious mind was as chic, as expensive, and as necessary as a family trip to Europe. It wasn't just our heads that they shrank. "Mr. Freud, Mr. Freud," sang satirist Tom Lehrer in the lament of a penniless patient, "how we wish that you were otherwise employed."

I went to my first psychiatrist when I was eleven, a larcenous suburban nymphet whose role models were Betty of *Betty and Veronica* and Emma of Flaubert's *Emma Bovary*. Every Thursday afternoon, while my fellow seventh graders were at baseball practice or glee club or learning to smoke Lucky Strikes in the bushes behind the football field, my mother drove me in the family Ford to Dr. Sobel's office in White Plains.

Dr. Sobel wore a tweed jacket and stroked a pipe as he pondered the mysteries of adolescence. He told me stories about being a psychiatrist—my favorite was the one about a patient who had attacked him with a chair—and I told him stories about being an eleven-year-old. He spoke to my parents, too; he told them I had a brilliant mind. "Whatever problems she may have in life," he said, "she has a Cadillac motor." Then he took my father aside and mentioned that my problems were not helped by my mother's irritability and hostility. That was just what my father wanted to hear; he thought my mother was irritable and hostile, too, particularly when they were having a fight. Soon afterward, my mother decided that I didn't need to see Dr. Sobel anymore.

That was in the fifties. In the decades since, I have been helped by loving therapists and yelled at by angry therapists. I have paid $160 an hour and I have been treated for nothing. I have been hurt by therapists and healed by therapists. At first, I had a tendency to think that my therapists were little gods. They knew me better than I knew myself. They were always right. They sat immobile and silent while I writhed with embarrassment and wept in pain. Through my tears, the gold lettering of their framed diplomas glittered on the wall. They seemed more like teachers than teachers, more like priests than priests, more like parents than parents. Often, I went to psychiatrists for absolution rather than advice.

It took thirty years of therapy with half a dozen psychiatrists before I understood what every patient should understand at the beginning:

these doctors of the soul, whether they are Park Avenue shamans or suburban, pipe-smoking gurus, are nothing more—or less—than professional men and women, some incompetent, some kind, some stupid, some remarkably gifted.

The next psychiatrist I went to was the redoubtable Dr. G. A white-maned Russian gentleman who practiced in his Brooklyn Heights town house, he was a former president of the American Psychiatric Association. He sat behind an antique desk sipping from a Canton teacup in a room decorated with rugs and a couch and a soulful portrait of Sigmund Freud. For angst-ridden 1960s intellectuals and bohemians, Dr. G. was the treatment of choice. He had treated many famous men and women, and sometimes—in the heat of therapy—he allowed himself to mention their names. Erudite, quick-witted, and educated in Britain, he was a literary father confessor whose patients avoided the stigma still sometimes attached to psychiatry.

Every Thursday afternoon, for many years, I climbed the steps to Dr. G.'s office—from the twentieth to the nineteenth century. My husband had been a patient of Dr. G.'s, but I soon took his place. Still, when my husband and I had a fight, Dr. G. would call him back in and scold him. My chastened husband bought me presents and apologized. I often wondered what our marriage would be like without the good Doctor. He was always on my side against the world, and I came to love him. When he told me that women shouldn't work, I believed him. When he said that women's concerns should be *Kinder, Kirche, Küche* I learned to cook and began to think about getting pregnant.

But our three-sided arrangement was doomed from the start. The Oedipus complex is only one of the many emotional Bermuda triangles that constitute the geometry of dysfunction. In retrospect, of course, I should have known that the Doctor, my husband, and I were a triangle that I disrupted at my peril. I went against Doctor's orders and got a job; other men began to interest me. It was then, as things in my life shifted, that the good Doctor started hugging me with his hand on my breast and kissing me on the mouth as I left his office—as if the thought of other men "doing things" to me, as he put it, was too much for him to bear. I needed him too much to confront him. I blamed myself for being cold to a man who had helped me. I started getting sick on Thursdays. I was often too busy to see him. I drifted away from therapy. I decided that a divorce would solve my problems.

In 1980, the publication of my first novel and the stress of a difficult love affair brought me to the edge of a nervous breakdown. It had been ten years since I had left Dr. G., years during which I had seen a few psychiatrists halfheartedly; now I understood enough to know I needed one big-time. First, I called Mildred Newman, a woman who was famous for her successful treatment of writers and for her well-stocked refrigerator. Mildred didn't have time for me; she suggested that I see her husband, Bernie. Hoping that the two of them at least shared refrigerator privileges, I went. But Bernie's soulful blue eyes and his certainty that I should leave the man I wanted to stay with unnerved me. At another office, on a stretch of Fifth Avenue dubbed "the mental block" because of the predominance of psychiatrists, a second doctor told me what my next book should be about—him! A third doctor, a tall man with a modern office furnished in pseudo-Eames chairs, asked me if I could introduce him to my literary agent.

Finally, I wandered into the office of Dr. J. He treated two friends of mine and was a man whose combination of professionalism and intelligence would save my life. In the twelve years I saw him—sometimes once a week, sometimes three times a week—he never faltered in his sympathetic redirection and explanation of my thoughts, feelings, and behavior. Three times in twelve years he told a joke. They were very good jokes. He never talked about himself. His support was always in the form of guidance. His mind and a bit of his heart were completely available to me; his body and his personal life were completely unavailable. The result was that I felt loved, but I also felt safe.

I went to Dr. J. to complain about the man I was in love with. He was indecisive, I complained. He was cheap, he was emotionally lazy, and it was taking him a long time to leave his wife. Dr. J. wanted to know why I was with such a man in the first place. He taught me to take responsibility—to stop worrying about how other people are going to act and why and to start worrying about how I act and why. He taught me that other people, even great psychiatrists, don't have the answers—I do.

I saw Dr. J. on the street the other day, running to catch a bus. At first, I thought he was just another New York suit, lanky and slightly stopped under the weight of a heavy briefcase, with the belt of his raincoat flapping loosely behind. Then I recognized him. Watching, amazed, I took in the fact that Dr. J., the man I thought was ten feet tall, who had the sex appeal of Robert Redford, the strength to cold-cock Arnold Schwarzenegger, and the savvy to out-quarterback Joe Montana, was really just a tired, urban, middle-aged man in a hurry—really just a brilliant professional and not a god at all. I knew then that my years in therapy were over.

DAVID MURA

AN INFINITY OF TRACES

It started with an oration. On a bench overlooking the mall of the University of Minnesota campus, in a place where I'd heard many such hyperactive speeches, I ranted about the marginality of poetry, its neglect by the masses and even by most educated people. I talked about the suicides of poets, Berryman off the bridge, the attrition and heart attack of Delmore Schwartz, dying alone in a New York fleabag hotel. If this was the fate of one of my literary heroes, who would ever read my poems?, I asked. Or care that I wrote them?

The quadrangle was empty on an early September evening. My only listeners were Dennis, a fellow graduate student, and Susie, whom I was living with and whom I later married. They laughed at my histrionics and answered briefly my questions about the hopelessness of my art, knowing my queries were merely rhetorical. I was on a roll, I could not be stopped.

What had prompted this outburst? A few hours earlier, Susie and I had attended the orientation day for her medical school. After a general introduction, I had gone off with the spouses and partners of the new med students. There we were told how busy our loved ones would be, how pressured, how little time and attention they would be able to give to us. We should prepare ourselves for this new rival and adjust to it. Perhaps, it was suggested, we might take up a hobby.

As I continued my speech on the mall, I recalled this suggestion with fury. I'd been placed in the position of the supportive but less interesting and less capable spouse, an adjutant to Susie's medical career. "Take up a hobby," I snorted. "Perhaps I should give up poetry for knitting." I told Susie how, when we had been sitting together with the new medical students at the orientation, I kept thinking, "My SATs are as good as anyone's in this room. Or better."

It was at that moment that something clicked. I knew I needed therapy.

Later, one of my group therapists, Rick, remarked, "You know, people don't simply sit on their lawn, drinking a beer, and suddenly think, 'There must be more to life than this. Maybe I need to go into therapy.'" He meant that the choice to enter therapy rarely comes in a time of peace and contemplation or simply from a notion to improve one's life. Usually, as Rick, an ex-barhound, would say, "It takes a lot of shit going down before people finally come in." The list of such "shit" runs as you might expect—depression, divorce, alcoholism, job loss, breakdowns, addiction, arrests, loneliness, failures, deaths.

My moment on the road to Damascus, my epiphany about therapy, seemed at first to be fairly lighthearted, more the beer-on-the-lawn-and-life-could-be-better scenario. When I started haranguing about SAT scores, I simply realized I needed to feel more secure about myself if I was to deal with Susie going to med school.

Then, too, I had been reading Menninger's *Man Against Himself,* with its series of case studies about individuals who, contrary to common sense, constantly went about damaging themselves. Some of the cases were quite extreme—suicide, self-mutilation, anorexia—but a few involved your garden-variety neurotics: intelligent and talented individuals who constantly thwarted their own ambitions, who always seemed to act against their interests. In these case studies, I found too many reflections of myself. I thought of how many times I had missed grant deadlines; of how I rarely sent out my poems to journals; of how I'd dropped out of grad school—or rather been drummed out—with seven incompletes; of how I couldn't finishing my writings.

But my failures with grants or with grad school were only surface manifestations. My problems went much deeper, far deeper than I was willing to admit at the time.

I'm a *sansei,* a third-generation Japanese American, and in my memoir *Where the Body Meets Memory,* I examine how the forces of race and sexuality worked together in the development of my identity. A large portion of the book deals specifically with the legacy of the internment camps in my family's psyche. But in the period just prior to entering therapy and, indeed, throughout the process of therapy, I did not see my racial or ethnic identity as crucial to who I was, nor did I connect these identities with the weather of my psyche.

All I knew was that the weather was increasingly dark and disturbed. Sometime when I was in my twenties, my circadian rhythms had become those of a depressive; I would stay up till the small hours and beyond. At times, these hours were associated with poetry writing; other times, they came with nights of prowling the bars, of increasing drinking and drugs. In recounting this period, I allude to a variety of obsessive sexual behaviors—masturbation, obsession with pornography, promiscuity (Susie and I had an "open" relationship, something I'd insisted on early in our history). Drugs and drink helped fuel the sex; these aids loosened me up, relieved me. I'd hit the singles bars on weekends or the two-for-one nights at the Cabooze, a blues bar. The nights I didn't pick anyone up, I'd move on to the porno bookstores, drunk and stoned, watching the 16mm on tiny screens in dank booths reeking of sweat and cum—quarter after quarter for five minutes more, like a gambling addict before a slot machine.

Gradually, this cycle grew endless, entropic. The hours I spent curled in my bed grew longer and longer; I was often there past noon, losing contact with sunlight, keeping a vampire's hours. I vaguely understood the connections between my feelings of failure and self-loathing and my behavior; that is, that my behavior was both a cause and result of these feelings, but this did not stop me. It only spurred me on, as if the drugs and sex might lead to a sense of oblivion or, if not, to a fall from consciousness, a dropping off from any ties with the world of daylight and regularity, responsibility and discipline, lucidity and rigor. My nights out grew more frequent, my bouts with sexual fantasies more compulsive, the hours of being stoned or hungover more sustained. Some part of me still viewed all this in a romantic tradition of decadence, the opium dreams of Coleridge; Byron's year in Venice with four hundred women; the manic affairs and drinking of the confessional poets like Lowell, Berryman, and Sexton; Baudelaire and the whores of Paris. An addiction to darkness and solitude and self-loathing, to closed shutters and sealed rooms.

No one really knew about this side of my life except Susie, who had to deal with the aftermath, my frequent bouts of melancholy, my eruptions of anger at her, at a world in which I never seemed to "score" as often as I desired, as I thought I deserved. Part of the time I played the role of poet and intellectual in grad school or with other writers; then there were my times alone out in the city, seeking some solace or fix, some way of quelling my consciousness, of easing my sense of failure, the sores of my soul.

As many with such problems, I led a double life. Light and dark. Jekyll and Hyde. Sober and stoned. In love with one woman, in lust with many. Grandiose and articulate; despairing and in a stupor. An intellectual and a writer; a wastrel degenerate. The weather of my psyche flickered back and forth between these poles, always pulling more and more deeply toward the latter.

Susie saw this polarity earlier than me. She felt her own complicity and despair, and turned to therapy. Initially, she tried a Freudian, but it was expensive, the woman said little, and nothing seemed to be happening. The Freudian did tell Susie that some of my obsessions might never be cured. After a few months, the insurance ran out.

Several months later, Susie visited a woman's therapy collective. The therapist wore long skirts, a shawl, a necklace of shells. She looked like a weaver, a clerk in a health food store. After Susie talked to her for forty minutes, the woman asked her about alcoholism in her family. Susie wondered at her presumption. A week later, her father entered the hospital with liver failure. A few weeks after that, he joined A.A.

Still, I desisted for myself. I'd been taught in my family that you solve your problems by yourself. You don't seek the help of others. All it takes is hard work. Or, as my father admonished so frequently as I was growing up, "You need to buckle down."

And if you were buckling under? For my father that was never an option; no such scenario was ever allowed.

There was nothing wrong with me. Nothing I couldn't handle. Or so I kept telling myself.

My therapist, D., had been recommended by Susie's therapist. I was twenty-eight; I judged him to be in his early thirties. He was a lanky man with thinning hair. In his recessed cheekbones, the stubble was already starting to grow back at four in the afternoon. He wore a flannel shirt and khaki pants. His eyes were dark and intense, a focused gaze that matched his earnest manner. There was, as I would discover, little room with him for flippancy or ironic banter. I'd later learn he'd grown up in Montana with a family that was, in the parlance, markedly "dysfunctional."

At our first session he asked me what I did, and when I told him I was a poet, he immediately responded, "Are you worried your being here is going to create problems with your work, with your creativity?"

I thought a moment. I told him I assumed we were there to ask questions, to look for the truth. That was part of my job as a writer; if I stopped doing that, it would harm my writing. So no, I wasn't worried.

This question about therapy's effect on my work was one of the initial moves he made to put me at ease. Another was to have me take the Meyers-Briggs test. At first, I told D. I felt skeptical about Jung; in graduate school I'd been instructed that Freud was intellectual and difficult, hard-edged and scientific, while Jung was soft and flaky. In the end, though, I was narcissistic enough to be engaged with what was revealed by my own psychological type. I was INFP—Introverted (as opposed to extroverted); Intuitive (rather than sensory); Feeling (rather than intellectual, although this was closer to the midline than my other scores); and Perceptive (rather than judgmental).

It turned out that this category was shared by certain poets and actors, those able to enter deeply into the characters they're portraying. I felt this reflected my tendency in my early poetry to write less about myself and more in dramatic monologues (my influences there were Browning, Frost, Robinson, Jarrell). Understanding my "type" allowed me to be more accepting of myself, the tendencies I sometimes saw as character flaws: I didn't mingle well at parties or large social gatherings; I had trouble at times making the smallest of choices. I now saw that these tendencies were accompanied by positive qualities. My introspection was very much part of my writing nature, the exploration of my own inner life. My lack of quick judgment allowed me a chameleonlike ability to embody the psyches of others in my writing; I could understand the complications of my characters and those around me in ways a more judgmental person wouldn't want to or be able to.

While the Meyers-Briggs profile probably gave D. some useful information about me, I think its main purpose was to start our process with something neutral, less emotionally charged and freighted with import. The hard work was still to come.

At first, we talked mainly about my parents, my childhood. I saw my father as a harsh taskmaster, constantly haranguing me, especially about grades, but also about any other faults he could find, from specific things—the way I mowed the lawn, the tackles I missed at my sophomore football game, the way I tended to mumble or speak with the inarticulateness of a high school jock—to larger issues: my lack of initiative, my unwillingness to work hard at things, my lack of moxie. Early on, the rules I had to follow were stricter than those of the other kids in the neighborhood. While my father wasn't violent, his temper could erupt anytime he was annoyed or when faced with my larger transgressions. When I was seven he whipped me with my Zorro whip when I came home with a note from my teacher about my talking in class; when I was seventeen and informed him I'd accidentally dented our LeSabre in a parking lot, he reared back and smashed me in the arm. At other times he'd threaten to take me out in the garage and smack me with a two-by-four. In his use of physical punishment he wasn't much different from some other fathers in the neighborhood. Still, I was terrified of him.

As I grew older, our differences increased. He was a Republican and once said the only good Democrat he'd ever known was Mayor Daley, who'd kept law and order in Chicago and ordered the police to move in on the antiwar demonstrators at the '68 convention. I was not only a Democrat, I was against the war and even had the audacity to say I was going to apply for a C.O. and, if drafted, would not fight in the army. I wanted to grow my hair long and did so my freshman year in college. When he picked me up at the end of the school year, he drove me straight to the barber. We ended up shouting at each other in the living room, where I declared, "I don't want to be depressed like I was all through high school."

To which my father replied, "I didn't know you were depressed."

And my mother said, "Oh Tom, you knew."

When I told D. about this incident, he asked how it made me feel. "I don't know," I replied. "I was angry, I guess." Still, what did it have to do with me now? Besides, at the time, everyone I knew was arguing with their parents.

Yes, said D., but how did this incident make you feel?

I started to answer, and he said to stop talking, to just simply let myself remember and feel that moment. What the hell good will this do?, I thought. But I sat there silently and tried to concentrate on what I was feeling. It all seemed a bit silly.

Later these moments of silence and trying to enter my feelings became routine. I got better at it. At first, there were simply moments of discomfort, then moments of confusion, then gradually sadness or anger or both. Feelings of abandonment and loss. Later I sometimes got to the stage of tears. Sobs. Pounding a pillow in an uncontrolled fury that found me screaming and wailing and left my muscles wrenched and sore.

I can see how someone from the outside might view this process within the clichés of therapy that are the source of humor in Woody Allen films or so many sitcoms or *Saturday Night Live* skits. These skits are funny to me, too. But perhaps funny in a quite different way than they are to those who haven't gone through this process.

Later D. helped me view that argument in our living room in a new way: my father had blocked out or denied how I was feeling in high school; he simply wasn't paying attention. My mother knew I was depressed, but never said anything. Either way there was nobody there who could help me understand what I was going through, what I was feeling.

Still, I wondered: what exactly did all this have to do with all my present troubles and depression?

In the beginning my own intellectual training led me to view the process quite skeptically. Eventually, though, I began to see its intellectual underpinnings and even to incorporate them into my own approaches to writing.

To put it simply, therapy views the family as a system. Within this system there are certain rules of behavior and perception: these rules determine how the individuals within the family are to react to events outside and within the family. In determining these reactions, the rules tell the members of the family which emotions can be expressed and how one is to express them. Since emotions are a fundamental way human beings understand or register the impact of the world, to deny them is, in part, to deny reality.

When a family system has broken down, it is often obvious to outsiders—especially when alcohol abuse is involved. But the members of the family cling to the system in part because it is the only reality they know; in an alcoholic family, the system does not allow the possibility of recognizing alcoholism as a problem. In terms of systems theory, then, the alcoholic family is a closed system: it does not allow for changes due to outside information. It is less adaptable, less true to the complexities of the world. It cultivates and encourages stupidity.

But what the system cannot completely suppress is feelings. True, it can deny the expression of those feelings; it can maintain that they do not exist, and can, eventually, so numb the members of the family that they seem totally alienated or unaware of their own feelings. As D. often remarked, depression isn't sadness, it's the repression of grief or anger or both. It requires a tremendous amount of energy to hold back your feelings, to keep them in check. If you try to hold down what you perceive as negative emotions, you can't let yourself feel anything else either. (No wonder depression leaves people drained and lifeless.) Your feelings are a form of intelligence; they tell you where the wounds are, what you've learned to forget or deny. In therapy your feelings can lead you to an understanding of the past and the ability to let go, and to break away from the family system.

Part of the purpose of therapy, then, is to make the client conscious of the unconscious rules of the family system and how those rules were formulated.

As Gramsci wrote in his *Prison Notebooks:* "The starting-point of critical elaboration is the consciousness of what one really is, and is 'knowing thyself' as a product of the historical process to date, which has deposited in you an infinity of traces, without leaving an inventory . . . therefore it is imperative at the outset to compile such an inventory."

What "traces" did my own psychological inventory, my investigation of my past, come up with? I noted an emphasis on work, accompanied by a denial of pleasure, a refusal to acknowledge any sort of balance between the two. I wrote about this later in an essay entitled "A Male Grief," in which I came to associate the puritanical ethic of my parents with the sexual obsessiveness that had grown inside me ever since adolescence:

There is often, inside the addict, a boy who did not learn the word pleasure. It lay like a stone on his tongue, hard, without taste, impossible to swallow. He was told by his father, work till evening, till the sun disappears and you pull the blinds, till the silence invades you, the silence which says the others have quit, have gone off to another life, are sleeping like animals, without conscience or law, without knowledge of the work to be done. And there will always be work to be done.

When sex entered the boy's life there was no word of pleasure to name it. It was sin, it was work. It was what kept him awake, deep into darkness, when the others were asleep. It was the secret that kept him ahead, outracing time. It knew no diversions, no wondering or wandering, no waywardness or waiting. It was a weight to be lifted, a grimness endured, a shield from the day, from the talk of others, their jokes, their meals, their music, their mundane lies. It used anxiety as fuel, a fuel always there and so to be trusted. It marked and measured, it drew from anger, it counted and counted. The list grew longer, it would never end, the tasks would keep coming. Exhausted at last, it let him sleep.

I do not know what he would have done had he known the word pleasure. It was where feeling might have flowed. It was kept a secret. It was kept for last.

Many of these connections and conclusions came later. In the early portions of my therapy, I simply talked to D. about my sexual desires, the hunger, the seeming need for woman after woman. I let him hear about the parts of my life I had told no one else about. In the atmosphere of our sessions and his seemingly nonjudgmental air, I saw no contradiction in driving from my therapy to the porno bookstores on Lake Street and there relieving myself of the tensions and work I'd just put in.

All that was about to stop, though.

You can make fun of the process, deride it.

The language it uses can be filled with clichés. A writer may wince at them and then, in therapy, be accused of hiding behind his intellect, pulling away from his feelings, riding a sense of superiority. In my therapy group there were no hierarchies. At one point, for a couple of weeks, I had to tell each member of the group why I felt superior to him. Then, one by one, the group was asked to respond. I left each session wondering, "Why am I paying all this money each week to feel like an asshole?"

Could I see certain great poets or writers upon the couch, draining the room with their narcissism? Perhaps. Rilke, Kafka, Joyce, Fitzgerald. But what about group therapy with its democratizing spirit, so dangerously close to reeducation? I can't see these writers allowing themselves to be broken down like that, asked to acknowledge with strangers a connection in misery, in childhood traumas, in their neuroses and depression, in their scars left by father and mother.

It's hard to see Virginia Woolf in group. Would it have saved her? Think of the airs she'd have had to let go. What would she have received in turn? The knowledge that she had been sexually abused as a young girl by her stepbrother, of the ways this abuse had shaped her feelings about herself, her relationship to the world. She might have had her perceptions about women affirmed, the need, the necessity for a room of one's own. Dismantling the patriarchy.

In its rational and sometimes binary labeling (functional/dysfunctional, abusive/healthy), therapy can seem to eschew the mysteries and complexities at the heart of great literature. Tragedy, for instance, is not commensurate with therapy. Therapy turns the tragic into denial, self-destruction, abuse, compulsive repetition. Foolishness and stupidity. Grandiosity. Addiction. Hamlet simply leaves Elsinore and his dysfunctional family situation; Othello in couples counseling either examines the sources of his jealousy and insecurities and learns to control his temper or else Desdemona leaves him; Richard the Third confronts his sense of humiliation and rage over his hump, his tendencies to overcompensate, and learns to be content with his station in life as a trusted brother and adviser to the king.

Imagine telling Kafka, For god sakes, Franz, your father's a controlling jerk. Stop giving in to him. (And what about your mother? Where is she in all this?) Look at yourself. You're no longer a child. You've got to learn to live your own life. Stop playing the role of a victim. Start seeing what you can do to change your life. Just move out of your father's house. (We'll save your sexual hang-ups for some later session.)

But the man who wrote *The Metamorphosis* didn't want to change his condition. He wanted to embody his dreams in singular and compelling tales. That was his compulsion. He had no other goal.

Most of us, though, are not geniuses. We have other goals.

At least some of us are simple creatures. We want to be happy.

A recent psychiatric study found that those who are depressed actually see the world and those around them more accurately and truthfully than those who are psychologically healthy and well adjusted—i.e., happy, content. In other words, to be well adjusted is to assent to a certain degree of denial.

And yet one of the most valuable things I learned from therapy was to stop thinking about what made me depressed. To stop obsessing over my relationship with my father and mother, the distance I felt from them, the ways I felt I had failed them, the criticisms I heard them making of me. After years of training I can now tell myself: Stop it. Stop this train of thought, these memories and projections. As my therapist used to say, they're simply a way of beating myself up. They lead to other self-inflicted character assassinations; what I used to believe was simply the truth of who I was, the truth I needed to face. Now when these voices of guilt and shame rear up, I refer to that old A.A. lingo: Let go and let God. Or simply: Let go.

The language is not eloquent or fresh. But it works. I stop obsessing.

Indeed, obsessing about my parents has become a signal to me that I'm getting depressed, my psyche's starting to drift or splinter. I need to talk to my wife and friends about what's troubling me. At other times obsessing about my parents simply means I need to recall and focus on all I should be grateful for, particularly my wife and my children.

I am simply happier not thinking about my parents. What this says about me as a son I'm not sure. What Franz Kafka might think about this I don't know. I know my mother has never forgiven me for writing in my memoirs about our family and the ways I view our family as a result of therapy. She believes such things should be kept private, secret, unmentioned. Eventually, they will somehow go away.

Out of all the children in our family I have moved psychically the farthest away (I'm also the farthest away physically: the two facts are not unrelated). My parents advise and criticize my brother and two sisters in ways they never do with me. They sense I've set certain boundaries between myself and them. I'd say this has helped me become independent and build a successful intimate relationship in ways I'm not sure my siblings have been able to do. My siblings might disagree.

Of course, this process of individuation—the therapeutic term—can't be separated from certain historical and sociological questions about our postwar era and the breakdown or breakup of the American family. But therapy isn't designed to answer or address these larger questions.

At least for me its purpose seems simple: to make your life a little better.

Or, for others and for myself, its purpose can also be: to keep you from killing yourself.

After the move from individual to group therapy, Susie and I entered couples counseling. In many ways this was the most difficult and painful part of the process. It was the place where I was confronted with the ways I had abused her emotionally, the ways my sexually acting out had hurt her, the anger she felt toward me, and the very real possibility of losing her.

Both my therapist and Susie's therapist conducted the sessions. "We're here," they said, "for you to break up or to stay together."

They explained that many dysfunctional couples simply stay

together out of inertia, out of fear and self-loathing, out of an attachment to each other's abuses and neuroses, out of an inability to imagine or consider another choice. The purpose of our couples sessions was to give us clear-cut choices. Maintaining the status quo was not an option. If both of us continued to work on ourselves, we might find a new way of relating to each other, we might heal our relationship. If we didn't, we should break up.

One of the first things that took place during these sessions was a simple and obvious step, though it didn't strike me that way: I had to stop seeing other women. Of course, I bridled at this, felt angry and victimized, felt I was being unfairly singled out. This feeling was exacerbated when I was told I also had to enter a group for "sex addicts." This was my equivalent of having to give up drinking, of entering A.A. If I did not comply, the couples counseling would end and Susie and I would probably break up.

I stopped my rampant promiscuity just before the AIDS epidemic hit. This choice might very well have saved my life as well as our relationship.

I won't go into much detail here about the struggles Susie went through to get to the point where she could confront me about my behaviors. She had grown up the daughter of an alcoholic. We met when she was seventeen and I was nineteen. She fell in love with someone who characterized himself as a loner, an outcast, a depressive, who needed the freedom to see other women, who required certain sexual outlets to ease his pain, as compensation for the unfair ways the world had treated him. She believed that she could save me, that it was her duty. It gave her a sense of being needed, a purpose. Without it she was nothing.

In these first sessions, she couldn't articulate all these things to me. Still, through the help of her therapist and mine, she began the process. Most often it was my therapist who confronted and pushed me, and her therapist who confronted and pushed her. This kept us from seeing each other's therapist as an adversary, an attorney for the other side.

Later I had to give up the pornography, as well as the marijuana, both of which had always been part of my sexual acting out. It was at this point that we began to examine the ways Susie and I related to each other, the ways our psyches meshed, our mutual interdependencies and how they affected the ways we argued. If Susie's goal wasn't to nurse or save me, what was her purpose in the relationship? If mine wasn't to be saved, if I had to save myself, what did I need her for?

We need to teach you how to argue, said our therapists.

But why? we asked. Isn't it better not to argue?

No, they said. Couples that stay together learn how to argue. But you have to learn how to argue fairly. To reach the real underlying issues between you.

Eventually, I learned one key source of our enmeshment: my job was to express the anger for both of us. Having grown up in a family where no one ever expressed anger directly, Susie was what our therapists called "passive aggressive." Instead of saying what she felt, she would engage in certain behaviors that expressed her anger and hostility indirectly. She would withdraw, hold herself back; she would forget to do things she'd promised to do or make decisions for both of us without my input. At a certain point, I would explode and become the wild man, the emotional abuser, railing at her. She would wonder what she had done, why I was so angry.

Through our therapists' help, I learned to pause when I began to feel angry. Instead, I would step back and simply ask Susie, "Why are you angry?" She would deny this. I would say I didn't believe her and point out her passive-aggressive behaviors. We would go back and forth for an hour, two hours. Gradually, she would begin searching her own psyche instead of asking me why I was angry.

And then suddenly she would explode. Often this explosion had to do with my behaviors in the past, with a whole reservoir of anger she had been holding back for many years. My job was simply to let her vent.

Over time I began to feel a sense of relief when she released her anger. It made things much clearer. Usually her reasons for being angry had a great deal of justification. I couldn't argue with them and, paradoxically, I felt then less angry, more at peace. All I could do was say I was sorry and listen. And later, when Susie finally reached the reasons for her anger, they sometimes had nothing to do with me, but with her own process, her own insecurities.

I dealt with my own problems in a very different way than Susie. During the early part of our relationship, I would blame her for my unhappiness or for not solving my unhappiness. But I learned there was nothing she could do about my insecurities or unhappiness. They were my job. I needed to solve them. The first step then was to learn to articulate them, to ask her simply to listen to me and from time to time give me feedback. It was important for me to keep focused on myself as my own problem solver and healer.

Though at times I would resist this process, especially if Susie asked what was troubling me, there were other times when I found immense enjoyment in trying to unlock my own psychic knots, a pleasure of discovery, a dialectic of questioning that both satisfied my intellectual curiosity and, in the process, seemed to relieve my symptoms.

In other words, I learned to work the therapeutic process on myself, with Susie or one of my friends as a listener and adviser.

But what of therapy and my writing?

To answer this, let me start with a bit of literary history. In 1922, T. S. Eliot met regularly in London for lunch with his friend and fellow poet Conrad Aiken. They would, as poets do, talk about their writing. Or, as sometimes happens, about not writing.

Eliot said that "although every evening he went home to his flat hoping that he could start writing again, and with every confidence that the material was *there* and waiting, night after night, the hope proved illusory: the sharpened pencil lay unused by the untouched sheet of paper."

One of Aiken's friends was a patient of the famous analyst Homer Lane, and Aiken told this friend about Eliot's problem. Lane said to his patient, "Tell your friend Aiken to tell *his* friend Eliot that all that's stopping him is his fear of putting anything down that is short of perfection. He thinks he's God."

Upon hearing this message from Aiken, Eliot was "literally speechless with rage" at both Aiken and Lane. "The *intrusion,* quite simply, was one that was intolerable." Eliot was a profoundly private individual and a man of great erudition and intelligence. To have several strangers aware of his personal difficulties with writing must have struck him as intensely humiliating, a breach of faith on Aiken's part and an uninvited presumption on Lane's.

And yet, Aiken believed that Lane's remark was well aimed: "It did the trick, it broke the log-jam." A few weeks later, Eliot traveled to Switzerland and in a short period wrote *The Waste Land.*

Neither Eliot's great learning nor his understanding of the literary standards of the tradition could solve his writer's block. What Lane offered him was a simple psychological truth about creativity.

Therapy was crucial in helping me to find a very different approach to the process of writing. As someone who was drummed out of graduate school with seven incompletes, I obviously had a problem with writer's block. For one thing, in my rabid pursuit of grades from grammar school on, I had learned to become a good student. Part of this meant that I always expected myself to be perfect: I knew I should never make mistakes or take risks, I should never fail, I should never question my teachers or write out of my own subjectivity, I should never stray from my chosen field of expertise, I should never look foolish or be silly, I should always take myself seriously. I needed to perform under intense pressure (indeed, that was the only way I *could* perform), and I needed to maintain absolute standards that I should never question.

Then I read William Stafford's *Writing the Australian Crawl.* According to Stafford, the secret to overcoming writer's block was lowering your standards. Stafford advocated a mind-set of openness and acceptance when approaching writing rather than one of performance and rigid competition. Writing, or at least creative writing, was a form of play—serious play perhaps—but play nonetheless.

Through therapy I learned that part of the reason I never finished anything in grad school was my subconscious belief that not finishing meant I still had a chance to make the work perfect. I also didn't have to take a chance on getting anything less than an A.

Stafford believed you have no control over whether the writing comes out "right" or not. Generally it's not. All you can do is enter the process, and you can't enter the process if you're not willing to fail or if you feel yourself pressured to perform according to some preordained impossible standard.

Writing, instead, is like the process of therapy. You start asking questions, you let your mind move where it seems to want to go. In other words, you learn to let go and listen to your subconscious. Or you learn to listen for the messages that bubble up from your unconscious. You or your conscious mind does not control the process.

The following is a scenario familiar to most writing teachers:

Each time a student brings work to show the class, the poems are all similar and all share the same faults. When the student is confronted with these faults, whether they be, say, an overuse of generalizations or sentimental language or obscurity, the student clearly balks at the criticism. He may say, "This is my style of writing," or "This is the type of poem I want to write," or "X read this and said it was wonderful," or "If I revise this I'll lose the original impulse for the poem, my true feelings," or any number of other defensive remarks. An argument may ensue in which the teacher-writer tries to use his or her superior knowledge of the craft to articulate more clearly the failures of the poem; in response, the student grows either more defiant or sinks in a morass of self-pity, embarrassment, resentment, and self-loathing. Whatever happens, it's clear the student does not want to revise the poem to any great extent. At this point, the question of whether or not the student knows how to revise is moot.

The desire is not there, so what good is any exposition on technique going to do?

What is the primary source of this impasse? Is it merely a lack of knowledge or learning or experience, all of which the teacher possesses to a greater extent than the student?

I would say no. The primary source of this impasse is psychological. Or perhaps even spiritual. This impasse occurs because of a set of beliefs the student has acquired and created over the years about himself and his writing. Very often, the student is not even aware of these beliefs or where they came from, but he or she will cling to them with great fierceness all the same.

In such an impasse, no one asks: What are the beliefs that propel the student's behavior? Where did those beliefs come from? What does their origin tell us about the usefulness and nature of these beliefs? Is it possible to create an alternative set of beliefs? What would these be? If we adopted these beliefs, how would our actions differ? How would our writing process change? What would this do to our identity and the way we look at ourselves?

When I teach writing, I want my students to examine their belief systems concerning writing and to see how certain beliefs are hindering their writing and how such beliefs might be changed. I think that many of the major problems writers face cannot be fully addressed through a discussion of technique. Indeed, it is often the case that a confrontation with one's own belief system is absolutely crucial to the writer's making further progress and unlocking his or her own creative powers.

In order to become the writer I've become I've had to move against the grain not only of my family but of the culture as a whole. On a personal level, I've had to learn the limitations of the role of the good student and to understand more cogently the process of creativity. Certainly therapy helped me in all these areas. The habit and value of moving below the surface, of trusting my intuition, of prodding the subconscious, of questioning the status quo, of letting the unconscious into the process of creation and revision, of radically reimagining my approach to a subject or piece of writing, of taking chances—I've learned a lot more about these in therapy than I have in my creative writing classes.

Given the way therapy is practiced in this country, it remains a middle- and upper-class phenomenon. It's not that lower-income individuals couldn't benefit from therapy, but it is an expensive proposition, and without insurance coverage, most people, especially those of modest means, will see therapy as a luxury they can't afford. As presently practiced, therapy generally doesn't delve into our society's economic and political disparities or the reasons they exist; it's rarely used to examine the "political unconscious."

If you're a person of color looking for a therapist of color, your choices are often limited. All my therapists have been white. Some might say this isn't a limitation; I would disagree. In my individual therapy, in group, in couples counseling, we rarely dealt with the fact that I'm a Japanese American and person of color. Japanese cultural norms; the effect of the internment camps upon my parents and their family; racism, especially my own internalized racism and the effects of the media and educational system—all these issues seemed to exist for the most part outside the parameters of the process.

How would a more politically conscious therapy view certain aspects of my family—the repression of feelings; my father's overemphasis on grades and rigid discipline; his fierce desire to be materially successful; the great need of my parents, especially my mother, to control their environment, to keep the house spotlessly, even obsessively clean? It might, for instance, ask how these were connected to the fact that in their adolescence my parents saw their families lose both their homes and businesses, that the culture and infrastructure of their community were destroyed, that they were kept temporarily in horse stables and then put in barbed-wire prisons for four years, that they were labeled spies and a danger to the American government? Or, more simply, it might ask how the repressions of these painful internment-camp memories are tied to other repressions in my childhood?

In therapy, we examined the rage I felt as an outsider and my seemingly uncontrollable desire to sleep with as many women as I could. Yet in retrospect, it seems very clear that, had I been brought up in Japan, my feelings about my own sexuality would have been quite different. As I was growing up, the only girls around for me to date were white, and every time I was refused I had to ask myself the following questions: Is she refusing me because of who I am as an individual? Because of the way I look? Because I look Japanese? Because she won't date someone of another race? Because her parents won't let her date someone of another race? Because she's worried what others will think of her if she dates someone like me?

When I traveled to Japan after finishing therapy, I realized that had I grown up there, the sexual wounds I might have incurred would have been quite different. I would not have grown up facing American cultural stereotypes about the Japanese and Asians; I wouldn't have found myself—from early adolescence on—consciously rebelling against the stereotype of the Asian male nerd.

After therapy, and prompted in part by my trip to Japan, I began to write more and more on the subject of identity and the history of Japanese Americans. In high school I would think it a compliment to be told by a white friend, "I think of you, David, just like a white person." As I came to see myself quite differently, I began to feel angry that my white friends were viewing me in this way. At the advent of the controversies over *Miss Saigon,* I fell into a number of arguments about race with several white writers I was close to. I wrote about these arguments in *Mother Jones* magazine. These issues, as well as my article, led to the breaking up of a series of friendships and my exile from the community of white writers with whom I had shared the experience of going through therapy. (Indeed, in those years, our mutual experience with therapy seemed a greater bond than our being writers.) However much therapy helped them confront issues such as divorce, suicide, sexual abuse, or alcoholism, they hit a wall of resistance when it came to race. One friend wrote to me, "You can write about your parents like this, but not your friends." With another friend, I asked if we could do a counseling session with his therapist over these issues. "No," he said. "I can't do that. I need him on my side." His therapist did encourage him to express his anger at my distancing myself from him. But apparently the issues that prompted our quarrels were peripheral. The real issue was not the racist stereotypes in *Miss Saigon,* or who controls the casting and representation of people of color in the theater and media, or the effect all this has on children of color; it was my friend's anger.

It's hard to imagine that racism would not be a central force in the psyche of many, if not most, people of color in this society. Not to look at its effect would generally be an act of denial. Would this be the same for most white people? Obviously, for most white therapists, as for most white people in general, these issues are not central. This has to affect and limit their ability to treat people of color, especially those who are not clear themselves about their own internalized racism. As to whether this also affects the ability of white therapists to treat white people, I obviously have my own answers to that.

Recently I was talking to two *sansei* who had read my books. One of them commented, "It's like your books are psychotherapy for our community."

Yes, I thought. A community that would rather not be in therapy.

In every social entity—a family, a community, a country—there's a desire to construct and hold to an idealized portrait of that entity. One task of the writer is to point out the falseness of that idealized portrait, to bring to light present realities and long buried histories that others would leave out or want to ignore. The writer is, or ought to be, addicted to truth, no matter how upsetting, no matter how much it hurts and disturbs, and if the writer is to carry out this dictum, he or she must be able to carry it out upon his or her self. You make conscious what your unconscious knows; you admit the unadmittable.

Therapy taught me to do this, to look into my struggles with addiction, with my family, in my intimate relationships, and acknowledge the untoward and ugly, the painful and destructive, the obsessive and the false. It taught me to ask that simple question, Why?, and then to keep asking that question over and over, uncovering layer after layer of answers, each leading to another. In my own mind the process eventually took on much broader implications than perhaps my therapist or the process we engaged in intended. For me, though, the sequence possessed a certain logic: You start with the individual psyche, then move to the psyche of your family, then to the social groups you find yourself a part of, and each time, you discover the rules you need to change, first inside yourself, and then, often, in the world around you.

As in many communities, therapy is not yet readily accepted among Japanese Americans. Aside from whatever cultural constraints might foster this avoidance, there's also the fact that we as a community are still invested in the image of ourselves as a model minority, as a people who experienced a great racial injustice and yet managed to survive and even prosper. We may have suffered but we were not damaged. In my own psyche, in my own family, I found the truth to be much more complicated than that, and from the stray stories I've heard among the *sansei* generation I know my own experiences speak to their experiences and their families, too.

I see my own struggle to understand and admit my racial and ethnic identity as both eccentric to the process of therapy and a result of it. Certainly the troubles that led me into therapy possessed a racial element, and part of my task as a writer has been to find a language to describe how race and ethnicity created and warped me. How did the emotionally repressive atmosphere of my family or my own lack of self-worth connect with the internment camps or with growing up in a society which promoted a culture of white supremacy in the ways we perceive our bodies, our histories, and our sense of who we, as a nation, are?

As a young poet, ranting about the devaluation of poetry and my own insecurities, years ago, just before I entered therapy, such questions were already there inside me. What I needed were the questions, the language, to bring them out. It's a story I'm still writing, essay by essay, poem by poem, play by play. What writers have always done—the therapy of the word.

SUSAN WOOD

NECESSARY CONVERSATIONS

An Essay on
Poetry and Psychoanalysis

The poem began casually, as poems often do. A warm September night in Colorado Springs, the front and back doors open to the mountain air. I turned on the television, my attention captured by a rerun of a PBS series, *The Way West*. The image that arrested me flickered on the screen for only a moment and then vanished, a nineteenth-century photograph of a family, a haggard woman holding a baby standing to the side in the foreground and, in the back right, a man and small children clustered by the door of a sod house, a single cow grazing on the roof. That's what I thought I'd seen, anyway, though I couldn't quite remember the composition of the picture. It was the woman's face I kept seeing, utter pain and loneliness, like an image imprinted on the retina when you've looked too long at the sun.

Perhaps where I was, and why, is important to the telling. I'd made my own way west to spend the month as writer-in-residence at Colorado College, working three hours a day with a group of exceptional student poets. Driving there alone, I'd experienced moments of panic as cars whizzed by me on the flat Kansas interstate. Gripping the steering wheel, I'd felt my own separateness from all those other lives in all those other cars, conscious that the body of my little blue GEO, as fragile as an insect's shell, was all that separated me from death.

This feeling was, I thought later, a manifestation of my fears of separateness, the way my unconscious associated that experience with death, something my psychoanalyst and I had been talking about for months.

There, in the furnished faculty apartment in Colorado Springs, I was glad to be away from my psychoanalyst, from lying on the forest green couch in her office trying to uncover the past, my past; glad, too, to be away from the daily distractions of my life, from the problems in my relationship with my lover. Of course, I was also afraid of being away, afraid to let myself feel how much I missed them both—the psychoanalyst and the lover—afraid of my solitude, but hungry for it.

Living alone for the first time in a while, I experienced a feeling of freedom. The apartment, on the third floor of a Victorian mansion, became my little aerie, my haven, a room of my own. From the back porch I had an unobstructed view of Pikes Peak, and I spent hours just sitting there, watching the play of light on the mountain, shading it from brown to blue to purple to black. And I wrote. The burst of creative energy that had begun the spring before and had seemed to wane over the summer now returned full force.

I'd never known that living in the presence of such extravagant natural beauty can make one feel awed and insignificant. In the shadow of Pikes Peak, I was aware of my own mortality as I'd never been before. I knew, really knew, as I moved uneasily toward my fiftieth year, that someday I would die, and the first poem I wrote in the mansion on Wood Avenue was about that consciousness, a feeling made manifest in my highway panic and somehow symbolized by an extraordinary week of weather in Colorado Springs that took us from summer to fall to winter and back again in a snap of the fingers. The second was a poem about the photograph.

What haunted me was not only the woman's face but also the space between the woman and the man, a space of only a few feet that seemed as wide as the Great Plains they'd crossed to get wherever it was they'd built their precarious house. Why had she stood apart like that? What had happened between them that made a few feet of dirt look to me like an unbridgeable chasm?

I had assigned my students a villanelle, the intricate nineteen-line French form that employs not only an A-B-A rhyme scheme but also requires the repetition of lines from the first stanza throughout succeeding stanzas in a strict pattern, a structure that makes it exceedingly difficult to meet the technical demands of the form while advancing the "sense," or content, of the poem. I'd never written one myself, but I had an impulse to try to write a villanelle about this photograph. Why? Though I've often told my students that instead of restricting them, form in poetry can make them do surprising things, can lead them places they would never, ever go without it, I myself had never experimented much with traditional forms. Recently, though, I'd been thinking more about them and had actually written what to me was a successful—and surprising—sestina the previous spring. Perhaps I simply wanted to see if the villanelle would surprise me, too. Besides, doing the students' assignment can be a good exercise for one's own writing and can offer insights for teaching. Or maybe the impulse for the poem was really this: that it was my own anxiety, somehow embodied in the pioneer woman's disturbing face and in the gap between the woman and man, that I wanted to contain within the walled formal garden of the villanelle.

The first line, one of the lines to be repeated, came quickly: "The mother, haggard, stands off to one side." The other repeating line I knew would have something to do with the gap between the woman and man that seemed as wide as Kansas itself, the place where I imagined the photograph had been taken, although I hadn't caught any of the particulars in the brief moment it had flashed on the screen. In my initial draft the line read "Miles away, though Kansas still—the gap's that wide—," but that line wasn't easy to fit into other stanzas. As I labored over technical problems, counting out syllables on my fingers, trying to make the poem flow by enjambing lines, devising rhymes and slant rhymes, I began to vary the repeating lines somewhat, still keeping the end words "side" and "wide" and retaining the sense of the woman standing apart and the gulf between the two people.

The story I imagined had to do with the original promise of their lives blighted by the vicissitudes of frontier life, a life that often brought death, particularly the deaths of children, and with the gap created by the different ways each parent might have responded to such loss. I imagined the grief on her face to be so utter, so private, that her heart had become sealed like a coffin: nothing could get in or out, not even the "baby floating on her hip like a cloud."

As I neared the end of the poem, though, I became aware of my own helplessness. After all, I'd only imagined this story; I couldn't really know the circumstances of the woman in the photograph. How can we ever know the experience of the other? Isn't the past lost to us, not just the past of history, but our own pasts, too? How can we know the truth of our pasts if memory always operates in the present and is constructed and colored by all that we desire, by our own subjectivity?

By the time I reached the final quatrain of the villanelle, the gap had become not just the gap I imagined between the couple in the photograph, but the gap between us and history, between the present and the past. The poem that began "The mother, haggard, stands off to one side" ended "The past is a chasm. That deep. That wide."

The anxiety in the poem, "Photograph, Circa 1870," was *my* anxiety, anxiety about "knowing," especially about knowing my own past, and anxiety clustered around the issues of connection and individuation, and of sexuality. To be connected to another must I give up my self? Where do "I" end and "you" begin? Do the differences between men and women create a chasm, a chasm that precludes their coming together in mutual respect and love? But that day in Colorado Springs when I finished the poem (or thought I'd finished it), happy to have solved the problems of the form, I didn't know yet how much of *my* anxiety I'd hidden inside it.

Back in Houston I showed the poem to a poet friend. There were things in the poem he liked, he said, but why had I varied the repeated lines so much? Somehow that was cheating, defeating the form. It would be more interesting, he thought, if I made what were now the first and last lines of the poem the repeated lines, and adhered to them strictly. He was especially curious to see what would happen to the poem if that last line—"The past is a chasm. That deep. That wide"— became one of the refrains.

I felt vaguely dissatisfied with the poem and decided to see what would happen if I rewrote it with his suggestions in mind. When I did, I found that the revised villanelle now emphasized the idea that the gap between the couple had occurred because of the different ways each of them experienced and evidenced grief. In this version, "the mother" became "the woman" and appeared even more passive than she had seemed, had in fact "died already," reduced to a "shadow," which was "fading even as we look," a view that also emphasized the writer's, and the reader's, distance from her and from the past. Perhaps it was really my own sense of powerlessness, my own depression in the face of a seemingly unbridgeable gap, that I was reading there: her face, instead of mine.

Still unsure of the poem, I showed this second version to a colleague in the English Department at Rice University. When he read the poem, he said, he kept thinking of Robert Frost's "Home Burial." I'd taught Frost's poem but hadn't been consciously thinking of it when I'd written my own. Full of the kind of sexual tension Frost often conveys with enviable subtlety, "Home Burial" depicts the conflict between a man and a woman as they survey the graveyard where their only child is buried, a graveyard that is framed in their bedroom window and that is itself "not much larger than a bedroom." The husband begs the wife to "Let me into your grief," but she refuses, angry at his inability to speak his own grief, furious that he could dig his child's grave and then come inside to speak of his "everyday concerns" that the rainy weather will rot "the best birch fence a man can build." She believes that "One is alone, and he dies more alone," that no one can know her grief, and she is angry at a world in which grief can be dissipated by time. "Home Burial" ends with the wife running from the house, the husband shouting after her, " 'I'll follow you and bring you back by force. I will!'—", the distance between them contained in that dash, the open space, which is the poem's final punctuation.

By now, my colleague said, that was a bromide, that men grieve silently, inarticulately, while women grieve openly, the unemotional masculine versus the emotional feminine. Did I really want to repeat that conventional assumption?

I'd had a vague sense that the poem still wasn't quite working somehow, but I hadn't yet been able to think clearly about it. I certainly didn't believe that men's and women's ways of expressing sorrow were so rigidly sex-defined. Didn't my own life prove that belief false, my own inability to express grief openly, to mourn my losses? When my mother had died eight years before, I had hardly shed a tear, terrified the tears would become an overwhelming flood in which I'd surely drown.

I resolved to rewrite the poem again, attempting to discover a less obvious reason for the distance I imagined between the man and woman. No matter how hard I tried to do that, though, the poem defied my efforts. I couldn't seem to think my way through the problem, couldn't imagine why the man and woman were so far apart.

One day I described the poem to my analyst and talked about the difficulties I was having with it. "Where exactly are you stuck?" she asked. I was stuck, I said, in the third stanza, stuck in a gap that occurred precisely at the point where I was trying to describe the gap between the woman and the man. There was a space there I couldn't cross. "Maybe," she said, "you don't believe that anymore. Not just that men grieve silently and women openly, but could it be you no longer believe that the distance between people is unbridgeable? Or between the present and the past?"

Gaps had brought me to psychoanalysis almost three years earlier: the gap between my "self" and my physical body, between me and others, between the present and the past.

Over the previous dozen years, my dreams had tried to tell me again and again that I was a house divided against itself. In one of them I was dressed in a nightgown I bought when I was about to be married in 1967, a year when young women—in the South at least—still thought in terms of *trousseaus* and *hope chests*. It was pink cotton trimmed in white lace, dainty and virginal. In the dream I was standing at the top of a flight of stairs and I was, quite literally, fighting myself. I was struggling with a figure who was my mirror image, down to the pink nightgown, except that when I looked into her face I saw a huge, overwhelming anger, her eyes silvery and murderous. I knew that I was fighting for my life, that she intended to kill me. Just as I was about to fall, I summoned all my strength and pushed her down the stairs. She lay in a heap at the bottom, facedown, unmoving, like a broken doll tossed away in a child's temper tantrum. I was glad I could no longer see her face. Waking, I felt frightened by how real the dream had been, disturbed as though I had actually been invaded by an alien being, and relieved to have rid myself of "her" rage. *I* certainly wasn't angry.

There was another dream, one that came more than once, always the same, dim but terrifying: I was lying in bed and suddenly, though I felt no pain, my head was severed from my body. I never knew where I was, how this had happened, why, only that it had. Always I woke up cold, disoriented, believing for a moment that I had literally come apart. I would reach up my hand to touch my head just to be sure it was still there.

Then there was the sleepwalking, something I had never done as a child. The first time it happened I woke up just as the elevator door closed. It took me a moment to realize where I was: in an elevator in the midrise condominium building in Washington, D.C., where I lived in the year after I separated from my husband, leaving our two young children with him, a place where I saw my children on increasingly chaotic weekends, the three of us crammed into an efficiency apartment whose only furniture was a gold sleeper sofa, a table and four chairs, a small chest, a bookcase, a TV. Waking, I left the elevator and walked back down the hall frightened by what I'd done, by the alarming feeling of being out of control. Relieved that the apartment door hadn't locked behind me, I went back inside, my heart racing. The sofa bed was still there, hard, uncomfortable, a bed of nails on which I lay each night drifting between my nightmares and the sounds of gunshots and police sirens, a kind of penance for my sins— my selfishness, my failure to love enough, the abandonment of my children.

This was the first time I was aware of walking in my sleep, although in the last year of my marriage I used to get up in the middle of the night to go to the bathroom, never fully awake, and fall back asleep sitting on the toilet, sometimes waking when my head hit the wall beside me. I did this night after night, though since I'd begun living alone I had stopped, only to replace it with a pattern of waking every hour on the hour. That was uncanny and exhausting, but the sleepwalking was terrifying.

A decade passed before I sleepwalked again. This time the back door slammed shut behind me. I was standing outside the large house where I lived on the Rice campus. The house was next to a residential college full of undergraduates, a house I occupied by virtue of my position as "College Master," overseer of these young people's lives. It was a position of great prestige at this university, where student life centered around the eight residential colleges. I was dressed only in a long cotton tee shirt, and there was no way to get back inside the house without alerting someone. It was spring vacation and few students were around, but what if I was seen like this, half-naked, disoriented? It would, I thought, undermine everything I'd worked for, my carefully cultivated position of authority, wisdom, sanity, responsibility. Haltingly, not knowing what else to do, I made my way around to the front of the house, to the courtyard that separated the master's house from the students' residence. Standing before the immense, heavily carved wooden doors, I suddenly remembered that my daughter was inside, home from her own university for spring vacation. I leaned on the doorbell for what seemed like hours until she let me in.

I never told anyone else about this incident, wanting to believe that it meant nothing, was an aberration, that it wouldn't happen again. I didn't want to believe it was a signal of distress from my unconscious because hadn't I worked hard to heal myself. Wasn't I a sane, responsible person? But it was really a metaphor for my life, the way I'd tried to hide from it, to move through it unseen and unseeing. To let things just happen to me. Not to feel. I was trying to walk out of my life, to let the door slam shut behind me, leaving me alone in the dark, where I was, where I belonged.

If a house divided against itself cannot stand, then I was falling over, not rapidly, but in a kind of slow motion that nevertheless would leave me in a heap at the bottom of the stairs. Over the years I smoked too much and from time to time I drank too much. Divorced for a dozen years, I had a series of brief relationships, the longest one with someone who lived in Florida whom I hardly ever saw. I had published a book of poems in 1981, but it had been a full decade before there'd been another, and although that second book had won prizes, I feared it would be a decade before there would be a third book, *if* there was a third book. I kept telling myself I didn't really have writer's block— that's when you can't write at all, and I was writing a couple of poems a year.

Still, it was becoming increasingly hard not to see—even for me— that I needed therapy. Again. Psychoanalysis had always appealed to me as the most rigorous of therapies—despite its current unpopular-ity—the one that seemed the most intellectually demanding, the one that took longer and went deeper, and over the years I'd read a number of its texts. Two friends who'd been in analysis urged me to go, not casually, the way one might recommend Thai food. They *begged* me to go. I claimed that I was too busy and that analysis was too expensive. Once, after I had the severed head dream again, I said I'd go, then went out and bought a dog instead and invested what seemed like an exorbitant amount of money in obedience training. Neither I nor the dog ever quite got the hang of it.

Finally, I ran out of excuses. Unable to disentangle myself from a destructive love affair and feeling increasingly out of control, I went back into analysis. It had finally become clear to me that all the old defenses, the old stratagems for survival had outlived their usefulness. If, as the British psychoanalyst Adam Phillips says, "psychoanalysis is a conversation that enables people to understand what stops them from having the kinds of conversations they want and how they have come to believe that these particular conversations are worth having," I returned to analysis feeling that all my conversations, with myself and others, were in danger of either falling into silence or becoming a jumble of indistinguishable sounds.

I remember the first time I went to the office—located (fittingly, when I think of the child I was) in a child development center—where I spent my first two years of analysis. I was nervous, my palms damp, misery tumbling out in a rush. I barely took in the office, its plainness, its slight air of dishevelment, its lack of expensive furniture or art, the sense it gave that important work was done there, work that left little room for adornment, the analyst's desk a jumble of papers and coffee cups, a bookcase containing the tomes of her trade along with a small rubber alligator and green plastic snake, the one picture on the wall a Georgia O'Keeffe print of a red, sexual flower, in a corner a dollhouse, a few children's toys, a little blackboard on which a child had drawn a smiling likeness of the analyst, chin-length bob, glasses and all.

I, too, felt like a child there. I sat that first day in the black leather chair across from hers and could barely look at the flowered couch on which I would lie for so many hours. I knew that I would have to learn over the weeks and months and years to give myself over to the process, to trust her, to crack the shell that surrounded me like a mummy's case, and I knew that it would be a struggle. The carpet stretched between her chair and mine, between me and the flowered couch, like an ocean.

In the weeks and months and years that followed, I lay on the analyst's couch and told my stories, over and over from different angles and different depths while she sat behind me in her black chair, her feet resting on an ottoman beside my head, writing in a red spiral notebook. What exactly did she write? I wondered. Did she take shorthand? How else would she remember everything? Listening, murmuring, asking questions, she interpreted myself to me as I brought my fears and wishes to consciousness, as I followed her down a path she'd already traveled. From the beginning she seemed to see through my false composure, my self-protection, to my deepest fears.

For me, the first risk of analysis was to entrust myself to her. Could she hear me? Could I allow myself to be heard? I remember a central moment toward the end of our first year together when I began to believe that the answers might be yes. Once, after a particularly difficult session, she bent toward me: "You think no one can not just know but truly appreciate, truly feel, the depth of your sadness," she said softly, right by my ear. And, of course, that was true. She had found my secret hiding place, the place where I tried to remain invisible. I lay there rigidly. "What if I can?" she whispered. "That would mean we're very connected." The recognition took my breath away.

I began to write again, not poetry but prose. Maybe, my analyst suggested, because poetry had always been such an unconscious process for me, writing prose was a way for me to work with more conscious material. I spent several months writing a memoir as a way, I think, of trying to give a concrete shape to what was happening in analysis. Or perhaps I wanted to master the experience rather than feel it—fix it, pin it to a board like a butterfly. The memoir didn't come to anything, really, never became anything I wanted to share with readers, and so I abandoned it as a long-term project. Maybe writing down my memories did in some way help make my unconscious more available, but that was already happening in analysis by that time. I'm not sure exactly what changed, but rather suddenly I began to write poems again, fifteen or sixteen over a three-month period, poems that were more emotionally honest, poems that seemed to integrate conscious and unconscious material in a different way.

Recounting your analysis is a little like recounting your dreams (to anyone but your analyst, anyway): it's too private and mysterious to be terribly interesting. And who knows exactly what happens in analysis or why. Just that you change, your feelings and actions change. It isn't just that you have bone-deep, shattering insights, though of course you do, those moments when the veil is lifted and you feel as if you've lived a lifetime in forty-five minutes on the analyst's couch. Other things come gradually, by inches. I, for example, learned that one of the central dramas of my life had been my relationship with my mother, a recovering alcoholic and an immensely bright woman who had never realized her gifts and had died of emphysema. I saw that in some sense I had never truly grown up, never become a separate self apart from her, even though she was dead and I was almost fifty; instead, I had taken on her deep despair, her unconscious desire that we be one mind and one body. But knowing isn't enough; in fact, for me, knowing—intellectual understanding—has always been a defense against feeling. Now I had to work through this insight in analysis and in my daily life, had to take the insight out of the realm of the intellectual into the one of feeling so that true connection to another would no longer feel like the annihilation of my self. That was the way I'd experienced the connection to my mother, and yet I had been desperate to maintain that merged state, unaware that real connection has room for both merger and separation.

At the point when my analyst suggested to me that perhaps I no longer believed that the distance between people was unbridgeable, I was struggling internally to take that step of separation from my mother. It felt like a struggle for my soul. It was December, nearing the anniversary of her death, a time when I had tended to act out in some self-destructive way the grief I couldn't express. I had just quit smoking again, aware that smoking was a way in which I kept my chain-smoking mother alive, in which I stayed merged, a place where I numbed myself to keep from feeling. As long as she was alive for me, not only could I not truly mourn her death but I couldn't live as a separate self.

The moment my analyst raised the possibility that I no longer believed what I'd been saying in the villanelle, I knew why I'd been having so much trouble writing it. She let me see the truth: I didn't believe that the gap between the self and others was an uncrossable abyss, nor was the distance between the present and the past. In the following days, I went back to the poem, determined to find out what difference that knowledge would make.

The villanelle, I saw, was too confining, too small, but I didn't want to get rid of formal elements in the poem altogether. I went back to the beginning: "She [not 'the mother' or 'the woman'] stands off to one side," I began again. As I worked on the poem—obsessively, of course—I found a form emerging from the ashes of the villanelle: three-line stanzas, ten to thirteen syllables a line, employing a rhyme scheme of A-A-B, C-C-B, D-D-E, F-F-E, and so on, most of the rhymes slanted ("door" and "moored," for example). Once I found the form, the poem seemed almost to write itself, circling and recircling around the distance I felt between the woman and the man and my inability to conceive its cause. A little over thirty lines into the poem, I decided to risk entering the life of the photograph to try to "read the stranger's face" in order to "translate her need and pain" so that "reflected in her eyes, I'm looking out at me looking back at her." But I remained conscious that the woman in the photograph and I were not the same: "The trick is to connect and stay apart, two solitudes communing." Once I saw her as a separate self, the "not-me," I was able to tell her story—or *she* was able to tell it through me—in all its particularity, a story that involved the pain of leaving behind all that was familiar to move west and the deeper pain of her children's deaths. After those deaths she could find no comfort in religion and imagined an immense nothingness, doubting everything but her own dreams. In one of them she had become a pitcher of water "so that when she opened her mouth, an ocean poured out." But she didn't drown in grief. The truth I discovered as I told her story was that she herself no longer remembered why she had stood apart that day. The moment in the photograph, after all, "had been only a moment in their lives." In the next instant, her husband reached out his hand and said her name and she turned back toward him, having come to believe that she would have drowned in grief without his love ("What could she do?/She loved him"). That was the thing that "seemed important to remember," the ongoingness of love and of life represented by the baby she carried in her arms. The poem—99 lines, 33 three-line stanzas—ends like this, the reader pulled back to the realm of concrete experience: "The baby she held was Anna. It was September."

After I finished the poem, I saw that I must have called the woman Martha after my mother, Martha Jo, who had been named for both her paternal grandparents, a pioneer couple not unlike the one in my poem. The baby's name, Anna, seemed to come to me out of the blue, though it was the name of my former mother-in-law, a woman I'd been fond of but never close to and who had died, I believe, feeling alone and abandoned, as unhappy as my mother had been, though for different reasons. Perhaps these names were a way of connecting these two mothers in my life. But both names, I realized later, are also directly related to me: for much of her pregnancy my mother had planned to call me Martha Ann, and the first syllable of Anna is the second syllable of my name, Susan, a form of the biblical Susannah. Certainly the poem enacts my connection to my mother as she is embodied in the Martha of the poem, enacts my wish for her, and allows me to make a kind of reparation by telling "her" story. It also enables me to mourn her loss by showing me that grief, like connection, does not destroy either the subject or the object. Through the poem I am connected to the past and, by implication, to the future in which I will be the past. At the same time, the poem establishes my separateness as the self who created it.

When I finished "Photograph, Circa 1870," I felt exhilarated and immensely grateful, as though the woman in the photograph really *had* spoken her story into my ear, just as my analyst had leaned toward me and spoke words of empathy and recognition directly into my ear. The poem was a breakthrough for me, not just in what I discovered but also in how I discovered it, allowing myself to let go and trust what the poem might have to tell me. It seemed to me, too, that the form of the poem was like what I was trying to find—or create—inside myself: a self that has its own individual form, but is fluid enough to change as it goes along. More than anything I'd written before it, this poem seemed to find a way to bring together the unconscious and the conscious, poetry and prose. Perhaps in speaking into my ear and in encouraging the birth of a new form for me, "Martha" was also representative of my analyst, though it wasn't until later that I realized how large a part she played in the poem.

Though I was excited, even giddy, about the poem, I experienced moments of great doubt. When I told a friend that I thought it was either the best poem I'd ever written or a complete failure, she commented that that wasn't like me, that usually I seemed so confident about my poems. Perhaps I'd finally risked enough to admit my fears, to admit to myself how much I cared. Or perhaps that doubt spoke of my anxiety about the hidden content of the poem. Most likely, my feelings can be explained by both.

Later, another friend, a photographer, told me that he thought he knew the photograph I'd seen on television and brought me a book of photographs by Solomon Butcher, a late-nineteenth-century photographer of the American West whose mission had been to document a way of life that was fast disappearing. The Butcher photograph he had in mind shows a family posed in front of their sod house, complete with a cow grazing on the roof. Rather than standing, though, the woman sits alone on one side of a table, while the husband and father sits on the other side, four children and two horses standing in a straight line to his left, a comment, perhaps, on the equal value they had as "property." Although there are watermelons on the table and the family appears to have been eating them, the woman does seem somewhat isolated from the rest of the family group by that table, but she isn't foregrounded as I remembered her. Her expression is more blank than pained. Most strikingly, I think, there is no baby in her arms.

When I first saw the Butcher photograph, I had a sense that I'd seen it before, even though it was so different from the one I thought I remembered. I'm still not sure whether or not Butcher's is the image that flickered across the television screen that evening in Colorado Springs; the picture I saw so quickly became *my* image, the one I wanted and needed, that I have no clear memory of it. The woman I think I remember is foregrounded in the picture just as my mother had been foregrounded in my past, as the analyst now is foregrounded in my present. And if the photograph that I saw didn't have a baby in it, maybe I needed there to be a baby in the woman's arms because *I* wanted to be that baby, both my mother's well-loved child and the analyst's. Perhaps I also sensed that both the analysis and the writing of the poem might be a kind of new birth for me, one in which I would have to look at the world through the child's eyes and might then actually grow up, become the individuated adult I had never really been.

I have learned other, more complicated things since then. Months after I had finished the poem and the first draft of this essay, I read them both at a conference at a local college. Afterward, a man who'd been in the audience said to me, "You know, of course, that Freud's daughter was named Anna and his wife was Martha." Of course. When I had been writing the essay, though, somehow I had "forgotten" this important information. Perhaps in choosing those names from the Royal Family of Psychoanalysis, I had unconsciously wanted to establish my connection to the analyst, to be both her child and her spouse, and perhaps I also wanted to supplant her, to be *her* creator, to be the analytic Father, the parent (of a daughter who was herself a great analyst, particularly of children), to be Dr. Freud himself. Still later, the analyst would suggest to me that perhaps I didn't so much want to supplant or replace her as much as I simply wanted to establish my own authority over my own life, to make myself its author. Certainly the fact that I repressed something I knew quite well—unconsciously chose to "forget"—seems, at the very least, to indicate that I felt anxiety about knowing my desires, whether the desire was to usurp or to accept authority or, most likely, both.

These revelations also led me to see how much the poem reflected not just my relationship with my mother, but my relationship with my father as well, especially in its earlier versions. It reflected my quite specific anxiety about an unbridgeable gap between men and women, about sexual difference, and about how that anxiety had had its origin in my difficult early relationship to my seemingly distant father, a relationship largely constructed by my mother. It also reflected other childhood experiences—including my mother's own unconscious feelings—which labeled the Male as Other, and the Enemy. Through the poem I could attempt to resolve that anxiety, to reclaim the Male, reclaim the Father, and reestablish my relation to the opposite sex.

It also occurred to me that there was something else at stake for me in writing this poem. One of the things that had been most difficult to face, to accept responsibility for and to forgive myself for, was what I saw as my failures at being a mother myself for, and I see now that I unconsciously felt that to acknowledge this would be to open myself to a grief that would be unbearable. Perhaps telling this grieving mother's story was a way to mourn my own failures and losses as a mother.

The poem performs another important function: It is a collaboration between me and my analyst—a literal collaboration, since it was her suggestion about the gap in the poem that led me to write the final version—and as such it represents analysis itself, a collaboration, a conversation, between analyst and patient in which, according to the psychoanalyst Thomas Ogden, they create something altogether new, what Ogden calls "the analytic third." The poem seems to represent such a creation, a kind of new "self," as it were, containing within it both the analyst's authority and my own.

I am in some sense all of these figures: the baby in the photograph and the poem, the child the baby will become, and the adult woman, the sum of all she will be. My "picture" is not complete, can never be, since one is always in the process of "becoming," and one of the chief insights of psychoanalysis is to reveal how much one can never know, how the unconscious will always surprise us, and even how we can take pleasure in that. Psychoanalysis gives one a new language with which to think, and through the language of psychoanalysis I have learned— am always learning—to speak my own language, the idiom of who I have been, who I am, and who I will be, and to be comfortable with, even to relish, the unknowable mystery of the self.

In the movie *Il Postino,* the postman tells the poet Pablo Neruda that "poems don't belong to those who write them but to those who need them." In this case I am both the one who wrote the poem and the one who needed it, and it is psychoanalysis, that ongoing conversation, that frees me to have the necessary conversations, in poems and in life, I didn't know I needed.

PAM HOUSTON

WITH NOTHING BUT
GRATITUDE

And she says, "Oh!"
And I say, "What?"
She says, "Exactly."
I say, "What, you think I'm angry?
Does that mean you think I'm angry?"
—Dar Williams,
"What Do You Hear in These Sounds"

Nearly three years ago, I got pregnant, went crazy, lost the baby, and had my computer stolen, in that order, and all in a very short time. Then I went on a fifteen-day cruise through the Panama Canal with my then boyfriend (the baby's father) and my dad. It was the darkest, most terrifying four months of my adult life, and I still shudder to think how close I came to going under. It was as if the whole series of events were designed by some universal force bent on ending my denial and promoting major change—a kind of *This Is Your Life* for dysfunctionals. It wasn't simply that the force wanted to dissuade me from any false sense of security I might have been harboring, they wanted to detonate it like a neutron bomb.

Prior to my pregnancy I had always existed around the edges of my occasional suicidal tendencies, which seemed in those days to be three parts despair and one part melodrama, a weather pattern I could step into and out of without ever really getting wet. If I was still asking the question *Am I suicidal?*, I always thought it was a pretty safe bet that I wasn't. This time, though, the darkness set in immediately and stayed, and I was immobilized by it beyond questioning. I was adrift in a black sea under a black sky waiting for a black wave, the one bigger than all the others, that would suffocate me, annihilate me, finish me off.

After two months of terror so intense I stopped getting out of bed in the morning (most days, even in the afternoon), it occurred to me to get back into therapy. I was still pregnant then and surrounded by people who said, *Of course, you won't kill yourself, you have another life inside you,* which made sense in theory, but in practice was another thing. My obstetrician said the same thing every time: *Mood swings are common, hang in there till the second trimester,* but there wasn't any swinging involved in my long, slow descent, and making it to the end of the day had become too much of a challenge for me.

I had been in therapy before, brief stints of it when I was nursing a broken heart, or having a hard time making career decisions. Those episodes had been all about self-examination and self-improvement, not survival, and I often had the suspicion that those therapists were having a hard time keeping up with me. I had always been articulate and self-deceiving enough to convince them that I deserved their stamp of mental health after only a few weeks or months of work, and I was always set free by them, all the darkest places in me still left unexplored.

This time was different. This time I sat quietly in the office with my lungs empty of oxygen and my limbs exhausted beyond use. This time I was so uncomfortable in my own skin I couldn't have come up with a lie convincing enough to fool anyone. With every breath I took I felt mild surprise that I was still alive.

Doctor L. had been recommended by a friend. He was exactly my age. Other than that, I knew nothing about him.

He looked at me across a hundred thousand miles of black water.

"Help me," I said, "save me, please."

And he took out his pad and pencil and said, "All right, I will."

I don't know how many hours we spent together that first day, but I know I talked for what seemed like forever, and then we went separately to lunch, and then I came back and talked forever again. I remember his pencil flying across the paper. I remember him drawing lines and circles and arrows like John Madden did on *Monday Night Football*. I remember being astonished at his ability to integrate everything I had thrown at him, the most random collage, his willingness to stay focused intently enough to take it all in.

By the end of that first day we had a plan about how to get through the next several. And though the work we would do together would demand more of me than I would have thought myself capable, and though we would uncover in those first few months a lion's share of grim details from a past I had mostly forgotten, once I started working with him there was never a single day that didn't feel at least a little better than all the days before.

I don't want to spend the words or the grief it would take to recount my personal history. Like all atrocities, the things that happened to me as a child were simultaneously profound and generic, and for that reason, as well as many others, I have not yet figured out how to tell that story on the page. And anyway, this is an essay about healing, not about the story that necessitated it. It is about the first person in thirty-seven years who gave me permission to tell my story, the first person who gave me permission to remember it, the first person who gave a voice to the girl who's always been drowning in that black sea.

I spent the first two months in therapy learning to trust Dr. L. enough to tell him the truth, at least the surface truth, at least what I thought the truth was before our work showed me that the truth was always a slippery thing. On the one hand this was easy. He was the only person available for trusting. He was the guy with the lifeline in his hand, but as he was quick to point out, I had made the choice against trust plenty of times before.

I have always thought of myself as a ridiculously confessional person, both in my life and in my work, but it didn't take long before I realized I was telling Dr. L. things I had never even thought to tell anyone, the stories I didn't even know I knew for certain, the stories no one could tell without being struck down dead.

Dr. L. presented himself with the perfect combination of intelligence and empathy; beneath that he had honesty and humor. I remember one day, early on, we were talking about the Tori Amos song "Silent All These Years." I was saying how I had always related so much to that song, though I could never figure out why, since it seemed like I'd done nothing but talk since the day I was born. "Right," he said, laughing, "you've been verbal all these years." We laugh a lot in that office, and about things you wouldn't even believe.

During our second session, we found out that we had both gotten perfect scores on the analytical portion of the Graduate Record Exam (GRE), which explained why he was the first therapist I'd ever been to who could stay one step ahead of me. What impressed me most about him in those first few sessions was that he wasn't afraid to back up and revise an earlier opinion, he was always quick to own his own issues, and he'd always tell me when he thought he might have been wrong. He said, *One day I'll say something really stupid and you'll look at me and roll your eyes and that will be a difficult day for both of us,* and that has happened in three years, but not very often. Although I now know he is only four or five inches taller than I am, that whole first year I literally believed he was seven feet tall.

This is probably not the best time to write this essay. It is possible that I should wait until I'm no longer seeing Dr. L. and I can see the completed arc of our process together, until I'm not so consumed with fear about violating it, until I've remembered everything I'm going to remember about my past and decided exactly what relationship to truth these memories have. It is somewhat dishonest, I know, to try to keep separate the past from the healing, and perhaps later I won't feel that necessity. I fear dishonesty more than anything, and yet I understand that I am capable of it, even sometimes in Dr. L.'s office, even here on the page where I'm striving for truth with all my might.

After two months of working together, I was convinced I had never felt safer with anyone in my life, and Dr. L. was convinced I was a post-traumatic stress victim. For both of these reasons, he suggested that if I survived the Panama Canal cruise, upon my return we should begin a therapeutic process of remembering called EMDR. In the seven days before the cruise, I lost both my baby and my computer, and you would have thought that would have given me pause, but out to sea I went like a lemming.

My father, my boyfriend, and I all slept in the same cabin—bed, bed, bed—like pigs in blankets, until the woman at guest services got a whiff of the tension and began, when she could, to slip me keys to vacant rooms. I spent the whole fifteen days in serious rope-a-dope position, and came home a little high on my own survival and ready for anything; it might as well be EMDR.

EMDR stands for eye movement desensitization and reprocessing. It is practiced by therapists in lieu of hypnotism or in addition to more traditional talk therapy, and I'll try to explain it the way it was explained to me.

There was a therapist at Stanford University named Francine Shapiro, who found herself feeling weighted down by the anxiety her patients were unloading on her. She went for a walk outside her office building, and spotted two birds chasing each other between a tree and a telephone pole. As she watched them, she was in tune enough with her psyche to realize that her anxiety was lifting, the longer she watched the movement of the birds, the better she started to feel.

This made her think of REM sleep, and how in dreams, which are brought on by rapid eye movement, our minds are given a chance to release our fears and anxieties. In dreams we process all the traumas, great and small, that we are not able to cope with as they are happening to us in the course of our week or day. She recalled the research that indicated that patients who are deprived of REM sleep go crazy in a matter of weeks, even if they have been allowed to sleep without dreaming. She hypothesized that if rapid eye movement could be re-created in a therapeutic environment with a post-traumatic stress victim who is lucid and awake, it might allow the brain to release memories that had not been previously available in the same way that dream images are released in sleep.

It wasn't too long after that that EMDR was born. In the beginning the therapist achieved the desired effect by moving her hand back and forth in front of the patient's face and instructing the patient to follow her. Some years later an entrepreneur invented a light bar the patient could sit and watch. By the time I was ready to try EMDR, doctors understood that the brain relinquishes its locked memories with any type of rapidly alternating right brain/left brain stimulation. I use headphones, a system as nonintrusive as a Walkman, with a simple alternating one-pitch tone in each ear.

Francine Shapiro believed that the psyche, like the skin or the bones, can knit and heal if the conditions are made ripe for healing. More important, even, than remembering the trauma is the reprocessing part of the equation. Once the trauma is set free from that enlarged and isolated place in the brain, all our adult coping skills can be brought to bear upon it. The remembered event stops being a monster under the bed and starts being what it is, something bad that happened a very long time ago.

I was terrified the first day I tried EMDR, not because of what I thought I might find lurking in my mind's recesses, but because of what I feared I might not. Dr. L. was fairly sure my trauma history was going to turn out to be ugly and extensive, and I didn't want to let his hypothesis down. By that time the combination of how much help I needed, how analytically able I was, how dedicated I was to my own survival, and how engaging a story I could tell had made me one of Dr. L.'s most valued patients, or at least that's what I needed to tell myself at the time.

I had visions of myself putting on the headphones, hearing the tones, and remembering nothing, Dr. L. waiting and waiting for some glimmer of trauma to flash across my face, and then finally, sadly, shaking his head. I would be an EMDR failure, I feared, someone who spent her life swimming in and out of the big black ocean just because she was too stupid to stay on land like everybody else. *She's melodramatic,* the ever-present critic in my head said, *she's a writer. We've always known she's been over the top.*

With all that noise going on in my brain, it's a wonder I could hear the tones inside the machine at all, but it wasn't two full minutes into the process before the images started coming. It was not unlike pushing a movie into a VCR, the slight delay and then the film's initial images, not coherent or chronological at first, but eerily precise, a dark and experimental tale filmed by some nihilist director and a cameraman with a love for the wide-angle lens. There were my mother's tulips, there were the tiny white stones that covered the log-landscaped steps down the back of a house that I would have said, had I been asked, I didn't remember. There was the clothes dryer where I hid from the mayhem. There was the oak tree the cat always climbed when the fur started flying inside.

The images came back, one at a time, eventually enough of them to form scenes and stories, more and more of them throughout that whole summer, some of them more gruesome than it would have been possible for me to imagine, some of them sweet and quiet and strangely light.

In the beginning I would tell Dr. L. about each image as it crossed my interior field of vision. As we got better at this he would wait until I had stories and scenes. We isolated three ages on which to focus, five, eight, and twelve, and three girls sprang to life out of these sessions and became so real to me that Dr. L. said he was the only therapist he knew who was trying to cure a patient of post-traumatic stress syndrome by giving her multiple personality disorder.

The five-year-old was the most accessible, the toughest, in a way, because she had not yet lost her hope, and she became our best source of information. The eight-year-old wouldn't come out of the dark for months, until I finally employed a tactic to get to her that I use in writing. I found a metaphor: horses, the thing she loved best, and we started with horse memories, drew her out with those, and worked our way back from there. The twelve-year-old is still mostly hiding, though she comes to me in moments. I haven't yet discovered the metaphor that unlocks her door.

The whole EMDR process is, in fact, so much like writing that for a while I got the two confused. When I write a story I start, almost always, with an image: a horse in southern Italy that wrapped his big neck around to eat green figs out of my hands, or the way the lines under the eyes of the man I love grow at once deeper and softer when he makes love to me right at dawn. I believe if I write the image truly enough, the meaning of the scene will rise up and out of it, will distill itself organically, and the story will be truer than anything I could write another way. It is the image, I believe, that knows the truth of the story, and if I have faith in it, it will lead me away from all the smoke and noise my conscious brain tries to use to control it, and deep into the heart of the story I'm trying to tell.

In EMDR, too, the images that lead me into the corners of my brain hold all the secrets, hold all the terror and pain. Like any monster under the bed, when they are brought to the light they lose some of their power, and become known, not by their reputation, but by their often diminished truth.

If writing is about taking the details that have been overlooked, and recognizing them for their profoundness, then EMDR is about taking the details that have been made too much of, and releasing them to a manageable size. In writing we try to find the truth that will make a story last forever; in EMDR we try to find the truth that will allow us to let a story go.

Until I did this work I always thought denial meant that you *know*, but you pretend not to. With EMDR I learned that it's really slightly more complicated, you really *don't* know, until you do, and that's when you realize that part of you always did.

When I would get a memory, especially if it was a particularly grisly one, I would tell Dr. L. about it, and we would revisit it again and again from every possible viewpoint. First, I'd be the little girl and then I'd be an observer. Eventually, I'd be myself grown up, the observer again, but big and strong enough to step in. You can see how this is like writing. I would revisit the scene from various narrative positions: first person past tense, first person present, third person limited, third person omniscient, everything from Nick Carroway's remove to Stephen Dedalus immediacy, we'd rewrite the scene using every trick in the book.

When it was over there was sadness, sometimes shock, but no longer terror. I was a grown-up. I could step in. I could save that little girl.

In time I came to understand that the right brain/left brain stimulation does more than just throw one image up at a time, though that is often the only way my brain can translate it. But sometimes, if I let it happen, I get a glimpse of my entire memory bank and how it all fits together. Sometimes I see a whole cross section of my consciousness, a layer-cake microchip kind of thing that I could have access to all at once if only I were smart enough. One day the chip handed me the entire 1980 Philadelphia Phillies roster, even the relief pitchers, and as far as I knew I hadn't asked.

I know it sounds simplistic, perhaps even moronic, but that summer, with the help of Dr. L. and EMDR, I learned to tell the difference between what felt good and what felt bad. It was not a distinction that I had previously been capable of, and once I was capable of it, it was the most profound experience of my life.

The girls—my five-, eight-, and twelve-year-old—went with me everywhere and helped me make decisions that would keep me moving toward the good things, and moving away from the bad. In between EMDR sessions, Dr. L. and I continued what I would call present-centered talk therapy, but when I was having some trouble resolving an issue, he would say, *Why don't you put the headphones on and ask the girls?,* and I would.

We used EMDR differently those days, as a tool to open up, not the memory exactly, but the imagination. We were talking one day about some trouble I was having with a friend in my life who had become a mother figure, and I found myself wondering if my mother hadn't died several years before, would I have confronted her with the memories that the EMDR had restored?

Why don't you do that, Dr. L. said, *go have a talk with her and see if any of the girls want to go along?*

I put the headphones on and asked them. At first, they all said no, but eventually the five-year-old relented. She said she'd come, but she wasn't going to say anything. She was just going to sit in her chair and watch what happened with her arms tightly folded over her chest.

My mother was my "good parent" and I seem to be married to that notion of her more than Dr. L. approves of, and more than the girls can tolerate. They are always skeptical when I propose a visit to her.

I called the meeting to take place in the last kitchen she had before she died. It was a house I had never lived in, so I figured we'd both feel pretty safe in it for different reasons. The five-year-old sat down at the kitchen table and I sat down next to her. We waited for my mother to settle in, but she kept shape-shifting into a big dark bird, a raptor of some kind—first an owl, then a hawk—and making big loops around the open kitchen/dining/living room. The little girl and I exchanged glances. *Give her time to settle in,* she seemed to say, *she's even more nervous than us.*

Eventually, she settled in, turned back into a woman, and I started talking, telling her the memories one at a time, starting with the most benign and working toward the most awful. My mother's face was set in the smile she reserved for my father and the camera. She was smiling too much and too steadily, and after a while the five-year-old reached over and pulled her face off and it turned out to be a mask, a Screen Actors Guild happy face in the image of my mother.

The five-year-old and I stared a long time at what was behind the mask. My mother was made of stone, her face had no features, just indentations for the eyes and mouth and nostrils. The five-year-old stood up and walked around the statue a few times and then, in a gesture neither playful nor violent, she toppled it out of the chair and onto the floor. It broke into several pieces, and to each piece she tied a balloon strong enough to lift the stone out the open kitchen window and into the sky.

You can see how EMDR is like dreams, and yet you can see how much it is like writing. More than either of these, it is like a miracle, and the day we tied balloons to my mother was just one of many days when I could feel myself getting better, one of the days when the girls and I left the office on the same page. Anyone who deals in miracles knows that one often leads directly to another, and it wasn't long before the next one. I'd be out in the real world, days or weeks from my last session, and I would find myself choosing the thing that would make me happy without forethought or hesitation, making the choice a whole person would make, without having to wrench my mind around 180 degrees.

Every writer knows that memory is a liar, that truth is a sketchy thing that only exists in metaphor, when it exists at all. When my then boyfriend wore my father's clothes on the cruise, I knew it meant that eventually he would leave me. When I saw the particular curve of the lines under my new love's eyes, I hoped it meant that he would not. When I saw my mother's face turn to stone behind my closed eyes in Dr. L.'s office, I knew more about her than I ever did while she was living. This is a writer's process, and I believe in it with everything I am.

Until three years ago I had almost no memories of my childhood. Now I have hundreds, but I'm afraid to say to anyone but Dr. L. what they are. I still can't say I'm perfectly clear about how much of it all really happened. I understand that this is part of the way my sickness protects me. If I didn't have denial in my childhood, Dr. L. has told me, I'd likely be dead.

One day after bringing to light a particularly brutal scene, I was shaking my head in disbelief and Dr. L. said, *See if you can understand this: Whether or not it really happened is less important than the fact that this is the way you remember it. Whether or not this really happened has very little to do with whether or not it is true.*

Could I understand this? I thought, *Is he kidding?* I thought of all the writing students over the years to whom I had said those exact words. I thought of how there couldn't be two other sentences that more precisely described the place I live in my head.

Dr. L. and I are well into our third year of work together, and our relationship continues to grow, though it has not always looked like a textbook case. He has been willing to see me at all hours, because of my erratic schedule (I think 6:00 Sunday morning before I flew to Patagonia was the most generous), and he's been understanding when I can see him three times in one week and then not at all for the next four. He's come to my rescue by telephone many times: once in France when he talked me and seven of my writing students through a kind of intervention, because the eighth student stopped taking her medication and became dangerous to herself and to all of us; more than once ship-to-shore when things got dicey in the Panama Canal; and once from the downtown Denver Post Office, on the night the boyfriend who'd worn my father's clothes broke up with me in the middle of a fifty-city publicity tour when I barely had enough energy in reserve to dial Dr. L.'s number. He compromised his boundaries once to go to a reading of mine at a local bookstore and that night gave me a rock from his office waterfall that I still carry, and I may have compromised him further by dedicating the book I could never have written without our work to him. Several months after that, I was sitting in his waiting room and overheard him say he hoped I didn't show up because he wanted to go running, and I almost snuck out forever without being seen, but he caught me with my hand on the door and turned the next two hours into maybe our finest session of all. He was the only person in my life who didn't say it was too soon when I met the man with the soft and deep eyes.

Above all, Dr. L. has shown me that I don't have to be afraid of my sadness. He has shown me that every time I act on my own behalf it makes me feel good. He tells me that I have never been in a better position to feel worthy of another person's love, and all but the very darkest places in me believe him. I have come to believe that he cares for me in a way that leaves me feeling nothing but safe and protected. I have come to believe that healing is impossible in the absence of that kind of love.

I am fighting the urge now to write a sentence assuring you that Dr. L. gets something out of our relationship, too, that I regale him with stories that delight him, that I have such an astounding ratio of breakthroughs per visit that I make him feel like he's made the right career choice, that our perfect-GRE-score minds link up so well that our sessions must at least sometimes be as much fun for him as they are for me. If Dr. L. were here, he would be quick to point out that this is one of the reasons I'm still in therapy, that I can't simply accept somebody's care and kindness without trying to balance the equation. He might also tell you that my need to perform for him, my need to find the right answer and get a gold therapy star, has kept our work, so far, from achieving all that it might. I have been more honest with Dr. L. than I ever have been with anyone, but I am still capable of lies of omission, I am still capable of trying to fool him with all the lies I tell myself.

But really, if he were here, he likely wouldn't tell you anything, because that's the rule of confidentiality, a rule I feel I've broken, even though I'm not sure it does or should apply to me. I'm still very much in this process, too close to have any perspective, too invested not to be overprotective, and yet the need to honor it, to honor him, to honor myself and all the courage on every side this process requires, led me to believe I should try to write this piece.

When our therapeutic relationship ends, if it ends, I will no doubt write a better essay. It will be filled with the things that make an essay good, the elegance of retrospect, the structural confidence that comes with a broader view. This essay is haphazard, born of nothing but gratitude, for a man and a process that have allowed me to be so much more fully alive than I could have dreamed.

The black waves are not gone entirely; they can still be called up when I feel particularly threatened, as they were just this morning, when I realized that for the first time since I've known my own history, I might be really, truly, deeply in love. I take solace in the hope that given all that Dr. L. has taught me I am making what he would call *proactive, self-caring choices.* I take solace in my newfound ability to distinguish the good relationships from the bad. More than any of this I take solace in the fact that love is terrifying no matter how good the choices, and I am a whole enough person now to step into the bright light of that terror, to understand the potential for loss and to take the risk willingly, to know that straight through the terror is the only path to the joy. The lines under my lover's eyes tell me that he knows all this and will soon show me more. I feel Dr. L. standing behind me, nudging me gently into the light.

LUCY GREALY

THE STORY SO FAR

Until I started seeing Ellen, I'd never spent more than six weeks at a time with any one therapist, the maximum number of sessions allowed by most college health plans. During those late teen years, I'd show up in the basement offices of the science building when the sheer momentum of my sorrow grew strong enough to carry me there. That was about it, though; I'd show up, start my story, then have to leave just when the story was starting to get good. Because I never got past the first few pages of my story, it was easy to think that what wasn't working about therapy was simply that: I didn't have enough time to tell the story. I drifted in and out of three different therapists' offices over the years thinking that what wasn't working was that no one ever got to hear the punch line.

I started seeing Ellen when I was about thirty, after I finally had enough money from publishing my "story," a memoir about having a disfiguring childhood cancer. I thought all my problems in life—trouble with intimacy, low self-esteem, the usual stuff—came from that story. Perhaps, some people have suggested to me, if I'd had therapy as a child I wouldn't need therapy now. These days, the idea of having a child wade through all that physical and emotional pain *without* therapy seems barbaric. I'm not sure how I feel about that. Instinctively, I think I'd prefer being left alone to being mishandled by a "grief counselor."

The reason I originally went to Ellen was that I was desperately lonely. I simply could not get myself into a relationship that lasted more than three months. My pet theory was that I was unlovable, and my thought was that I could use therapy to "improve" myself, make myself more lovable. Whereas my stabs at therapy in college had failed because I couldn't find the right person and/or situation in which to "tell" my sad story, I could now afford "real" therapy and would be able to untangle the mess of my life. All it took, I thought, was finding the right person to listen to me.

I went to two therapists while I was living in Provincetown, Massachusetts, attending an artists' colony for the winter. The first therapist had interesting tattoos on her face, and asked the last names of people I was talking about. At the end of our first and last session, she announced that I should know she had a husband and a wife.

"Maybe you've seen my husband around town; he's got tattoos all over his body?" I *had* seen her husband; he was one of the local topics of conversation.

"And my wife, Carol, is a tattoo artist."

"Cool," I said.

The next therapist wore, at our first session and last session, a sweater with Porky Pig cartoons all over it.

I finally met Ellen when I moved to New York. She struck me as smart and straightforward, and I began telling her my tale of woe. Now, I thought, I could finally tell my story properly.

What I didn't know was that my time in Provincetown had set a different type of story in motion. A story about stories, maybe, or maybe a story about writing, or maybe just a story with no clear beginning and ending. It started with a phone call. Let me tell you that story:

The first time he left a message, I just knelt there on the carpet, staring intently at the answering machine. His flat voice asked me to call him, leaving only a name and number, and I suspected he was a bill collector. I was continuously in debt and had instructed myself to start screening calls. He phoned once more when I wasn't in, and left another message, a slightly more specific one that mentioned Tennessee. Two days later, he called again when I was in. I sat on the blue couch, perfectly still, while his voice groped blindly through the magnetic tape, afraid to move, as if I'd give myself away.

Provincetown, the tip of Massachusetts's Cape Cod, was my home that winter. I was writing my memoir, which I did not yet know would eventually bring me a kind of low-volume success. My apartment, which I rented for only fifty dollars a month, was right on the water, offering itself up to any and all bad weather. To me, this was the best feature of the apartment: the wind howled so dramatically I had begun to speak back to it, while the whole building, a three-story house, swayed enough during a storm that I could see the water in my toilet bowl slowly sloshing back and forth. This was true of the water in the bathtub, too, a place in which I spent copious amounts of time. I was heartbroken that winter and the steaming water I lowered myself into each night felt like the only thing willing to hold me, that had any patience at all.

Despite the rest of the year's heartbreak, that Christmas was the best I'd ever experienced, primarily because I was putting into action a rule I'd discovered in graduate school: be nowhere near your family on holidays. I roasted a turkey and invited everyone I knew. With my small apartment stuffed with friends who kept letting the toilet run and the indoor cat outside by mistake, I was happy. I was so happy and involved that when the phone rang, I picked it up without hesitation.

"Hello?"

"Is this Lucy Grealy?" the dreaded voice asked.

It was the bill collector. I was caught. In that split second, I thought how it was a dirty trick to trap someone on Christmas: I imagined him stealing my name from some application form.

"Who is this?" I asked.

In the next split second, I made a sudden delirious decision to get

my life back in order. I would fess up, pay my bill, and then, as if bid-
den by this good deed, everything else that was good in the world
would march right into my life.

"Are you the daughter of Desmond Delargy Grealy?"

The vision of the glorious new order in my life vanished. I had not
heard the full, three-tiered name of my dead father spoken aloud in
many years. I'd said it myself a few times, the answer to official questions under the fluorescent light of insurance company offices, but I
had not heard it said by a stranger since his funeral, fifteen years before.

"Yes," I told the man on the phone.

"And are you the sister of Sean Grealy, and of Nicholas Grealy, and
Susan Grealy?"

"Susan? I don't have a sister named Susan. Who is this?"

"What is her name?"

"Who the hell is this?"

He told me. I don't remember his full name now, but his story was
this: My brother, Sean Delargy Grealy, had fathered a daughter named
Margaret eighteen years ago. Now this Margaret Grealy had hired
him, a private detective, to find out everything he could about her
long-absent father.

I faltered for a moment before speaking.

"I hope I'm not the first one to tell you this, but Sean died in a car
accident, a little over a year ago. Or, actually, we found out a year ago:
he'd already been dead for a year. That makes it two. Two years my
brother's been dead."

The irony had been that a year ago I'd been on a plane, flying back
from three years of living in Scotland, and on that flight I'd had the
morbid fantasy of having to tell my mother about the death of Sean
from AIDS. He was a long-term heroin user, and I figured this had to
be his ultimate fate.

After my plane touched down at Kennedy, I went to visit my
brother Nicholas, nine years older than me. He buzzed me into his
apartment, but waved me into silence when I entered. He was on the
phone, having an intense conversation. When he hung up he told me

it had been a friend of Sean's, that she'd been trying to find Sean's family for the last year, to let us know.

The first thing we had to do was call my mother. I sat with the phone on the floor in Nick's narrow hall, smelling the smoke of his cigarettes embalmed into the plastic handset, and listened to my mother cry. She told me something then I'd never heard before: that of all the children, I was the one who resembled Sean the most. Not only in the way I spoke and thought, but even in the way I moved, the way I walked.

When I was growing up, Sean had been the great taboo subject in my family: speaking of him upset my mother so much that we simply didn't. He'd been an angelic-looking child with a high I.Q.; a true golden boy, a favorite son. Then adolescent-onset schizophrenia was diagnosed, and then the drinking started, then the drugs, then he left us all for good to go live three thousand miles away.

My mother would sometimes get into strange moods and talk about Sean. Before I knew how to recognize the signs of drinking, I thought it was the talking about Sean that put my mother in her mood. She'd take me to her room, sit me down on her bed, and explain how she had loved Sean the best, and how he had broken her heart, and how that was why she didn't, couldn't, love me. I sat there on the edge of her bed, hands between my knees, and nodded in empathy.

Despite all his problems, Sean, from what few clues we received, had retained an almost uncanny charm. His friends loved him, remained loyal to him, no matter how often he harmed them. "I can see that in you, too," my mother told me on the phone, crying with the news of his death, "not the illness, but the charm, the way you have with people: you're just like Sean."

Sean was thirteen years older than me. By the time he left home, I was just learning how to remember. With only childhood pictures to guide me, and exactly one photograph of him when he was sixteen, I grew up with only a vague, ribbony idea of what Sean looked like. If he'd walked into the room and sat beside me, I would not have recognized him.

My family had known about Margaret's existence from her birth. We even had a tacky shopping mall–style portrait of her, the fake trees in the background, the blue blanket she lay upon meant to represent a babbling brook. But Sean left her and her mother when Margaret was small, and we'd never heard from either of them again. There was another child, a boy, named Lennon or Lenin, and another girl, named either Melissa or Michelle, and maybe even another son. Each of them remains a rumor: we have never looked for them, and only Margaret looked for us.

Though I had very little to tell this private detective, a few translucent memories, I agreed to speak to him on one condition: that he send me a copy of his final report.

For the ten years before I wrote my memoir, I'd been a poet, surviving on air and fellowships at writers' colonies. I understood that becoming a poet was not financially rewarding. My almost accidental entry into the comparative riches of prose changed this: suddenly, writing was not only the thing I did with my life, it was the way I paid my rent.

This changed me in subtle ways, some of them good. When I first sold the rights to my book, before I'd actually written it, a friend warned me, "You better get a therapist." Except that we were in the middle of a heat wave, with the fans on high and the windows open, the traffic blaring below. I thought she'd said, "You better get a hairpiece." This made perfect sense. Of course, I would need some sort of disguise. I was about to reveal so much.

The notion that writing a memoir would have any cathartic effect on *me,* of all people, was utterly silly. *My* writing was about the larger truths in the world, and had nothing to do with pop psychology. Whenever anyone asked if I thought it would be a "healing experience" to write my story, I felt vaguely insulted.

My reluctance toward anything that employed the verb "healing" had to do with an instinct that not only abhorred reductionism for aesthetic reasons, but simply didn't believe healing was possible. Healing, as in "made all better," as in "gotten over," as in "over." Nothing was ever over, as far as I could tell.

While actively writing poetry, I'd developed an incredibly rigorous aesthetic, one that involved an almost religious honesty about specific moments, about rendering them as truly and clearly as possible. Having a preconceived idea of how a poem or image was going to work was a sure way to produce a terrible poem, or a forced image. One had to watch carefully how an image developed, learn to listen to it, be prepared to change one's expectations of it whenever it strained, like an adolescent, against the expectations of how it *should* behave.

Though I didn't have the language to describe it, or even the desire to perceive it as such at the time, my student self's relationship to art was decidedly conservative. Narrative was my form of choice, though I often chose to mask it within the lyric; even when my images or topics were abstract, the way they flowed from one to another within a poem still described a fairly straightfoward emotional journey. What I didn't yet understand was how complicated even the simplest narrative is (because at heart the act of narration requires faith in a rational world), how complicated my own life already was (though I wanted to believe it was simple), and how much more complicated it would yet become through my attempts—spiritually, emotionally, rationally—to understand it.

Despite my deep-seated belief that there were certain things I would always suffer from (a low self-esteem, a belief I was ugly and unlovable), writing my memoir did help me close the door on some of my insecurities. How? Because my loyalty was to my writing. Writing was how I learned to be loyal: I'd never considered this virtue in regard to myself, or been given ample chance to apply it to anyone else. I was determined to produce not an account of my own victimhood, but a respectable piece of writing. The only way to do this was to apply the same rigorous aesthetic honesty to my *life* that I'd previously applied to abstract images and themes, to language. It was only when forced to place my own life under the microscope of my aesthetic that I realized two important things. One: I'd undergone an extraordinarily difficult set of circumstances, something that in my attempt to diminish and normalize those circumstances, I'd previously never been willing to admit. And two: I'd done not only well, but very well, considering those circumstances.

The process by which these revelations arose was simple on the surface: I had to go back and mentally, emotionally, reinhabit my past. Simply, I had to remember what happened. Oddly enough, when people later asked me about this remembering process, they asked in a tone that implied I had undertaken a great effort, that I had somehow painstakingly gone back and researched, rebuilt my story, detail by painful detail.

In truth, it was not a building process, but a disassembling one. I did not have to go seek the details, I simply had to allow them to come to me. This involved placing myself in a state of mind that invited them back; that, in turn, involved leaving all my judgments and preconceptions behind. Because what I found to be the greatest obstacle to remembering wasn't the effort itself, but the insidious nature of memory—how it confused itself with interpretation. How I *thought* about a particular event, how I felt it affected my life, interfered with my ability to remember the event itself clearly and purely. It was almost like reading a review of a movie before seeing it. My mind wanted to direct my attention to particular details and insist they were meaningful, when, in fact, they might actually have seemed inconsequential at the time, or might have had a significance completely different from the one they would eventually accrue. A comment my mother may have made in passing, the way all our cats seemed to run away, the particular love of privacy and freedom I found alone in my musty basement bedroom.

After my book was published and I began seeing Ellen, I recognized the two processes as essentially similar. An absolute loyalty to the truth was required, a letting-go of how I had come to think it was all *supposed* to be. Still, without doubt, and without my recognizing it, my greatest obstacle in therapy was the notion that I was somehow supposed to reconstruct a set of childhood memories that would explain, highlight, or at the very least underscore the problems with intimacy and self-doubt that haunted me as an adult. Once I did this, told the right story in the right way, I felt that my problems would be exorcised like so many ghosts from an otherwise desirable house.

I still thought it was about the story, the narrative. Without my real-izing it, popular culture stoked this belief; Hitchcock films such as *Marnie* and *Spellbound* insisted it was the simple act of remembering the forgotten that led to curative wholeness, while even seemingly innocu-ous television programs, such as *Gilligan's Island* and *Bob Newhart,* based whole scripts on the idea that single past events shaped entire lives. Once again, it was the act of conjuring up these buried events that brought resolution and order, even if only comedic order, to one's life.

Despite a snobbishness that ruled out the idea that I could be affected by popular culture's reductive interpretations of complex the-ories, I still believed Therapy, with a capital *T,* was all about the heroic act of remembering well enough, of finding the right story with just the right touches of pathos, cruelty, and indifference to explain the rather mundane emotional mess I'd found myself in.

My memoir was finally finished and published. People I hadn't heard from in years called to congratulate me. People I only dimly remem-bered, and some that I didn't remember at all, contacted me. One phone call came from a woman I had never met: she wanted to know if the Sean Grealy in my book was the one she had known in high school. After an exchange of verifying details, I told her yes, then told her the news of his death, which hadn't been part of the book. She broke down in tears. Awkwardly, over the long-distance call, I tried to console her.

Some weeks later an envelope appeared. It was late morning when I fished it out of my mailbox, which meant it had actually arrived the day before. It was a large manila envelope. So much time had gone by, so many things had happened, that I'd forgotten. It was from Tennessee.

The private detective's report was eighteen pages long. Most of it covered my brother's life after he'd left home, when I was quite young. All these details about his life, things I'd neither known nor, I have to admit, ever really thought about. The names of his friends, his girl-friends, where he spent his time, the sad accumulation of details, cul-minating in his falling out of the back of a pickup truck at one in the morning after the driver, a man named Peter, hit the base of a bridge while making a right-hand turn.

I sat there on my rug and read all of this: a stranger's life. And then, when I turned to the last page, I saw it was a photocopy of my brother's death certificate. His name was right, and there were the time, place, and reason of death: massive head trauma. Also, that he had lived 0 minutes after the injury. I didn't know there was space for that information on a death certificate, but it made sense that people might want to know such a thing. I hoped that the coroner—I'd never even used the word "coroner" before, it belonged to news reports and detective novels—was right about that zero. It made it easier.

But under every other heading on the death certificate—birthplace, age, occupation, father's name, mother's name, address, education, categories I didn't even know they put on a death certificate—typed in lowercase letters, the same word, over and over and over again: unknown, unknown, unknown, unknown. I lay down on the carpet and wept.

Then I realized it was time to go meet a friend. I cleaned myself up and solemnly went out the door, checking my mailbox on the way. The mailman was just leaving. In my box was a fat, white envelope with a return address I didn't recognize. I didn't know it as I took it out of the box, but it was from Sean's old high-school friend—the one who had broken down on the telephone. She was sending me photographs she had taken twenty years ago, a yellowing set of pictures of Sean when he was sixteen or seventeen.

As I said, I'd only seen one picture of Sean when he was that age. What I haven't said yet is that I only have one picture of myself from that time. I hated cameras, and successfully avoided them for the most part, except for one photograph my older sister had taken of me when I was about sixteen. In it, I am sadly turning my head toward the camera, looking big-eyed and melancholy but smart. I remember hating it at the time, but I had recently looked at it again. Maybe it was just youth, but I saw in myself a certain grace and beauty, despite the fact

I'd thought myself obscenely ugly at the time. I'd been wrong, I understood, when that picture of myself resurfaced. I hadn't been ugly at all.

Walking down the street to meet my friend, I opened the other envelope, still not knowing what it contained, and then stopped there on the sidewalk when I saw the top photograph. It was of Sean, in a pose exactly like the one I had in my own photo. My mother was right; he looked just like me. The same forehead and cheekbones, the same eyes, the same hair, the same oval face, the same sad grace.

I walked into a bar in Greenwich Village. My friend was already there. I walked to the table she'd gotten for us, tossed the envelope filled with the photographs and the envelope with the report onto the wooden surface and said, There: look at that, and you will know exactly as much as I do about my brother's life.

As a poet, I'd lived a life in which romantic notions of truth and beauty and posthumous fame tempered the realities: a credit rating in the negative numbers, the knowledge that I would never qualify for a mortgage or a credit card, the possibility of never living in one place longer than the average one-year term of an associate professorship— none of these things seemed too terrible. Perhaps it was simply that I was young. Perhaps I felt on the brink of something.

The truth is, I *was* on the brink of something. Publishing success. My memoir, coaxed out of me by an agent and an editor, had given me more money, and more opportunities to make money, than I had ever earned as a poet. The money from the book kept me afloat for three years by itself, while the opportunities to write magazine articles, teach at well-endowed schools, and apply for larger, more prestigious grants all suddenly dropped into my lap. Abruptly, I could afford an apartment in New York City. I could afford to fulfill a lifelong dream: I threw out all my clothes and bought an entirely new wardrobe. I traveled. I ate dinner in restaurants, and discovered I could distinguish a thirty-dollar bottle of wine from a four-dollar one.

This wasn't a rags-to-riches story. I had not lived in poverty before, only a poorness as outlined for an educated white person, which essentially meant that previously I had to take the subway instead of cabs, owned not a single stock, and, as I said, was a failure on the abstract yet reified scale of credit rating. I'd always been aware of my privileges and my opportunities, an awareness which, no matter how many bill collectors I was avoiding, still highlighted the chasm separating my relative poorness from the debilitating poverty experienced by fully two thirds of the world's population.

Yet, once I tasted of the comparative riches of my own society, once I learned I could make good money by writing, something changed in me. It's not something I'm proud of. I began assessing subjects in terms of whether or not I could sell them as ideas for a book or an article. This is not to say that I turned into a money-grubbing fool, but this much was true: I learned how to calculate things on a scale of worth that I'd never previously considered.

So, when I told some friends and a few editors about receiving this private detective's report and the photographs in the mail, they all wanted me to write the story. Maybe just an article, maybe I could get a whole book out of it. I could travel out to California and retrace my brother's steps, reinhabit his life so that I could learn something about him. This could be connected to the larger themes of what it means to have a family, what societal trends my alienation from my brother acted as a paradigm for, what directions of healing might be gleaned from my own individual journey back to my brother. It sounded good. Everyone thought so.

Except for one problem. It was baloney.

Maybe, though, I could make it true. Maybe, by the very process of seeking out the facts, by putting myself through the experience of obtaining the narrative details of my brother's life and then observing, reflecting upon, and writing about that experience, I could learn something true about my relationship with my brother. After all, I never expected any "healing" to come from the process of writing my memoir, so why was I balking now?

I'd never been much good at prose before I began my memoir, but I learned the craft of it while blundering my way through the book.

Now I was not only well paid to write prose, I actually *taught* it to people; people who looked at me expectantly, wanting not just the secret of writing, but the secret of success. Previously, I'd taught only poetry courses. There, not many people planned on getting huge advances for their books. And even if the majority of my poetry students didn't go on to live their lives as poets, at least I knew I had given them—or attempted to give them—something that transcended material notions of career: the knowledge of language, the intimacy of its powers, and its beautiful, instructive failures.

In my nonfiction classes, the most pressing problem was my students' belief that the story itself mattered above all else; in their opinion, the writing was secondary. Not in mine. Most classes were dedicated to showing this, trying to get them to believe that even eating a cheese sandwich could be an exciting, profound act if written well enough. But their beliefs persisted, encouraged by the books appearing on the bestseller lists: badly written accounts of interesting lives. My cheese sandwiches and I got left in the dust.

It was the Enlightenment that opened the doors for Freud, the idea that reason could ferret out the truth. In the centuries previous to the Enlightenment, much of medical science believed that each body's disease was individual in origin, definition, and cure. There were as many diseases as there were bodies, and this belief helped medical practitioners maintain their strong aversion to research and descriptive observation—why waste time developing a theory of how the body, or one of its diseases, worked, when it obviously did so in an entirely different manner for each individual? It was only as late as the early part of the eighteenth century that doctors began to consider the value of studying and describing the various organs and their functions in any systematic or organized manner, and, by doing so, allowed for the new and surprising fact that diseases often ran fairly predictable paths through most patients.

Freud listened to each of his patients' personal stories, and fit them into a universal template, the various stages of human development. Each detail of a patient's life, no matter how particular and personal, pointed toward a larger abstract framework. Recognizing how their own sordid details fit into the subtleties of this larger truth was the only way, Freud believed, that his patients could begin to seek freedom from the pain associated with those details. And in the midst of all this scientific language, the actual heart of the process, the thing that was both diagnostic tool and therapeutic treatment? The telling of a story.

Memoir is all around us, in every nook and cranny of our culture, from the bestseller lists to daytime talk shows. Perhaps the overwhelming success of the narrative nowadays—pure narrative, without the art of telling featured as a part of the story—is in part some strange leftover symptom from Freud. Regardless, these stories pour out of us. They never stop, because they never run out.

But the larger truths our particular details might signify are more difficult to discern. What do all these stories mean? Before the Enlightenment, religion gave us the framework for our stories, which always underscored either our virtues or our sins. The Enlightenment gave us the idea of human development, which—though Freud never intended it—hinted that everything was fixable. Now either there is no larger truth, or we simply can't get to it. Either the moral majority is right, and our world is in decay because of our lack of "values," or money really *is* the root of all evil, and has stripped us of the ability to say the truest thing. Perhaps we have forgotten, or have not yet been able to articulate, the newest version of what art means to us in this post-Enlightenment, postreligious time, and that is why we can't find the story that finally says it for the last time. Or, maybe, it's always been this hard.

Going from being a writer of poetry to a writer of prose meant, in essence, my transition from attempting to convey small moments of being that held within them the suggestion of larger moments of understanding, to attempting to convey understanding that resulted from the parceling out of relevant information at particular intervals. Add, on top of this, my realization that I could actually make money doing the latter. I did not necessarily have all of this in mind while I was writing my memoir, but subsequent to its publication I could feel that the way I moved about in the world, the way I perceived it, had changed.

My problems in therapy persisted. I often wondered what the hell I was doing there. I felt a strange pressure to be confessing things while in that room, or at the very least remembering in a heroic, tearful manner.

"I can *see* how the dynamics of my relationship with my mother get repeated in my relationships now, but I just don't get how that realization is supposed to *change* anything," I complained to my therapist.

"Why is it supposed to change anything?" Ellen asked back in her typical therapist-speak. I was always accusing her of therapist-speak.

"Well, if not, then what is the point of retelling the story? I mean, I just can't buy the idea that I'll stop feeling so lonely and unloved by recognizing that someone in my past allowed me to feel that way. I mean, I feel lonely because I *am* lonely."

I thought that therapy was trying to sell me some notion that my negative emotions were containable and controllable; that I was not in a relationship because somehow I engineered it that way, or that I secretly didn't want to be in a relationship. Why couldn't my therapist understand that I was not in a relationship because I was deeply flawed and no one wanted me? Why did she have to be so hardheaded about it? I sincerely thought that she believed that if I could get the narrative of my early childhood straight, I'd recognize my barriers, walk out into the street, and find true love in the first single, appropriate man I met (as opposed to the unavailable, inappropriate men I was always pining for). "Hogwash," I told her.

"Hogwash? What's hogwash?" she asked.

"That it's my *subconscious* that doesn't want me to have a relationship. I mean, really."

"Is that what I said?"

"Isn't it?" I asked, tentatively.

When the story, or the facts as I had them, of my brother surfaced, and then the possibility of writing that story for good money followed, it was yet again my own sense of aesthetics that forced my hand. The possibility of uncovering the "truth" of my brother's life was seductive, but I could not give in to the temptation. Because another true part of *this* story, the one I am telling you now, is that I had already told a story, the one I told in my memoir; and another true part of *that* story is that it doesn't even tell the secret, saddest story of my life, which I'm saving for a future memoir. In the artificial but useful hierarchy of the sadness of things, Sean's story holds a distant fourth.

Or perhaps I am kidding myself. Perhaps the simple, precise, and thus elegant trauma of my mother telling me she did not love me because I was, and was not, my brother is the genesis of all my troubles. Evidence for this: the very first poem I wrote that worked, that *clicked,* was when I was a freshman in college and I wrote a poem called "My Brother." In the poem I say not one true thing. None of the poem's particular details of searching for a lost brother are true. I made them up. But the larger desire that drives the poem, the desire to find something, someone, *anything* that will tell us we have found our home, is as true as it gets.

I can't point to the moment in this story when therapy actually began to help. Sentences flow in a necessarily linear manner, but whatever self-understanding I've gained through therapy has come about in a circular, roundabout path that would bore the pants off any reader if I tried to write about it. What is boorish and hackneyed on paper can be profound and life-changing in reality. Luckily, however, life has offered me one particular metaphor that contains within it the possibility for comprehending, all at once, my relationship with therapy, with my brother, and with my writing, and might possibly explain why I will not write, will not put into boorish and clichéd language the plot of my brother's life. It is not a story about a single instance, but a repetitive one, a story that happens over and over, almost always the same in basic plot.

I always knew I had a brother out there, somewhere, and that he was probably, in some way, suffering. I knew he was mentally ill, I knew he was a drug addict, I knew he was sometimes homeless. But because I didn't know any of the facts of his story, the form of my acknowledging Sean's existence could not happen in any linear way, and so came to me instead in those small moments of interchange that always offer the experience of deep understanding. I'd like to call these moments Poetic, but that label, with all of its attached meaning, would suggest something sickly sweet, a Made-for-TV act of healing. I'd like to call these moments Symbolic, but that suggests a culmination of meaning and experience that is transformative, and I balk at that notion because it, too, suggests some kind of resolution. Simply by writing about these moments I am, in form, forcing them into a Narrative; but no, that isn't it, either. Sometimes the form of a thing *is* the thing, and sometimes it's only its shadow. I don't know how to tell you about these moments except to tell you about them.

These moments happen on the street, often in doorways. They are actually a bit clichéd. It's not hard to give money to the sad, fallen-on-hard-times-looking homeless in New York, but I know people find it difficult to give to the obviously drunk and threateningly erratic. Though it resolves nothing, and perhaps means nothing, I have never had a problem opening my wallet. There is no larger narrative intruding, nothing warning me for my own personal safety, or suggesting that I am perpetuating this person's problems, or this society's problems, by accommodating a sordid need when I hand that person on the street a stray, pitiful dollar, and that person, whom I will *never* meet again, takes it.

ABOUT THE

CONTRIBUTORS

Diane Ackerman is the author of five volumes of poetry and nine books of nonfiction as well as a play and media adaptations. Her most recent books include *A Natural History of Love, The Rarest of Rare: Vanishing Animals, Timeless Worlds,* and *A Slender Thread.* Her work has appeared in several anthologies including *The Norton Introduction to Literature, The Norton Introduction to Poetry,* and *The Paris Review Anthology.* She has received the John Burroughs Nature Award, the Peter I. B. Lavan Award from the Academy of American Poets, among others, and was also nominated for a National Book Critics Circle Award. Currently she is Visiting Professor at the Society for the Humanities at Cornell University.

Douglas Bauer's books include the novels *Dexterity, The Very Air,* and *The Book of Famous Iowans,* and a nonfiction account of a year of reunion in his hometown, Prairie City, Iowa. His newest book, *The Stuff of Fiction: Observations and Advice on Elements of Craft,* is forthcoming. He teaches in the Bennington College MFA program. He has received grants from the National Endowment of the Arts and the Massachusetts Artists Foundation. He lives in Boston, where he is at work on a novel.

Susan Cheever's nine books include five novels and two family memoirs. She teaches in the Bennington College Writing Seminars and at Yale University. She is a contributing writer for *Architectural Digest* and writes a column about parenting her two children for *Newsday*. She is working on a book about raising children as well as on a biography of William Griffith Wilson.

Mark Doty is the author of five collections of poetry and two memoirs, *Heaven's Coast* and *Firebird*. His work has received the National Book Critics Circle Award and the PEN/Martha Albrand Prize for Nonfiction. A Guggenheim and NEA fellow, he has also received a Whiting Writers Award. He teaches half of each year in the graduate program in creative writing at the University of Houston, and spends the remainder of the year in Provincetown, Massachusetts.

Adam Gopnik is the author of *From Paris to the Moon, Wayne Thiebaud: A Paintings Retrospective*, and *High & Low: Modern Art Popular Culture*. He is a staff writer at *The New Yorker*.

Emily Fox Gordon's essays and stories have appeared in *Gettysburg Review, Boulevard, Southeast Review, Salmagundi*, and the *Anchor Essay Annual*. One of her essays has been reprinted in *Pushcart Anthology XXIII*. She is the author of the recently published *Mockingbird Years: A Life In and Out of Therapy*. She lives in Houston with her husband and daughter.

Lucy Grealy is the author of the memoir *Autobiography of a Face*. She won the National Magazine Award for an excerpt from *Autobiography of a Face*, published as "Mirrorings: To Gaze Upon My Reconstructed Face" in *Harper's*. A collection of essays will be published in the fall of 2000. She is currently at work on a novel.

Pam Houston is the author of *Cowboys Are My Weakness: Stories, Waltzing the Cat,* and *A Little More About Me*. A native of New Jersey, Pam now resides in Jensen, Utah, where she writes, teaches, and is a hunting and rafting guide in the American West and Alaska.

Phillip Lopate has written three personal essay collections, including *Against Joie de Vivre;* two novels, *Conference of Summer* and *The Rug Merchant;* two volumes of poetry, *The Eyes Don't Always Want to Stay Open* and *The Daily Round;* and one book of movie criticism, *Totally, Tenderly, Tragically.* He has also edited several anthologies, including *The Art of the Personal Essay, Writing New York,* and *The Anchor Essay Annual.* He is on the faculty of Hofstra University and Bennington College. He lives in Brooklyn with his wife, Cheryl, and daughter, Lily, and sees his therapist, Barbara, in Manhattan.

Carole Maso is the author of *The American Woman in the Chinese Hat: A Novel; Aureole; Ava: A Novel; Defiance: A Novel; Ghost Dance; The Art Lover: A Novel;* and *Break Every Rule: Essays on Language, Longing, and Moments of Desire.* She currently teaches at Brown University.

E. Ethelbert Miller is the editor of *In Search of Color Everywhere.* His most recent book is *Fathering Words: The Making of an African American Writer,* a memoir published by St. Martin's Press. Mr. Miller was recently the African American Studies scholar-in-residence at George Mason University. He is the director of the African American Resource Center at Howard University.

David Mura is a poet, creative nonfiction writer, critic, playwright, and performance artist. Mura has written two memoirs: *Turning Japanese: Memoirs of a Sansei,* which won a 1991 Josephine Miles Book Award from the Oakland PEN, and *Where the Body Meets Memory: An Odyssey of Race, Sexuality and Identity.* His two books of poetry are *The Colors of Desire* and *After We Lost Our Way.* His book of critical essays, *The Limits of Our Vision,* will soon be published by the University of Michigan Press in its "Poets on Poetry" series.

George Plimpton is the author of over twenty-seven books of fiction and nonfiction as well as several anthologies, which include: *Writers At Work: The Paris Review Interviews; The Bogey Man; American Journey: The Life and Times of Robert Kennedy; Sports! An American Biography; The Paris Review Anthology; The Best of Plimpton; The Norton Book of Sports;* and *Truman Capote* as well as being guest editor of *Best American Movie Writing 1998.* He founded *The Paris Review* and has been its principal editor since 1953 and a contributing editor for *Sports Illustrated* magazine since 1967.

Ntozake Shange is the author of over fifteen plays, four novels, seven volumes of poetry, and three books of nonfiction. Her titles include *For Colored Girls Who Have Considered Suicide When the Rainbow Is Enuf, From Okra to Greens: A Different Kind of Love Story,* and *Nappy Edges.* She is the recipient of a Pushcart Prize, a Lila Wallace–Reader's Digest Annual Writer's Award, a New York Drama Critics Circle Award, a Paul Robeson Achievement Award, and a Guggenheim fellowship. She currently teaches at the University of Houston.

Rebecca Walker's work has been featured in such magazines as *MS., Harper's, Cosmopolitan,* and *Vibe,* and in various anthologies. Her latest work, a memoir, will be published by Riverhead Books in 2001. She lives in Berkeley, California.

Meg Wolitzer is the author of *Surrender, Dorothy, This Is Your Life*, and three other novels. Her short fiction has appeared in *Best American Short Stories 1998* and *The Pushcart Prize 1999.* She lives in New York City with her husband and their children.

Susan Wood is a professor of English at Rice University in Houston. She is the author of two books of poems, *Bazaar* and *Campo Santo,* which received the Lamont Prize from the Academy of American Poets, and has recently completed the manuscript of a third. She is the recipient of fellowships from the John Simon Guggenheim Foundation and the National Endowment for the Arts, and her poems have appeared in the Pushcart Prize anthology and *Best American Poetry.* Another essay on her experiences in psychoanalysis, "The Tornado in the Carpet," was included in *How We Want to Live: Narratives on Progress in America.*

COPYRIGHT NOTICES